THROUGH
AN ADDICT'S
LOOKING-GLASS

First published in 2023
by Hajar Press C.I.C., London, United Kingdom
www.hajarpress.com
@hajarpress

ISBN 978-1-914221-20-0 Paperback
ISBN 978-1-914221-21-7 EPUB eBook

A Cataloguing-in-Publication data record for this
book is available from the British Library.

Cover and interior art: Han Gunji Stephens
Cover design: Samara Jundi
Typesetting: Laura Jones / lauraflojo.com

Printed and bound in the United Kingdom by
Clays Ltd, Elcograf S.p.A.

THROUGH
AN ADDICT'S
LOOKING-GLASS

WAITHERA
SEBATINDIRA

*For Stacy, for whom I'd have built a new world
with my bare hands if I could.*

Contents

PLAYLIST

Bill Withers – 'Grandma's Hands'

Amy Winehouse – 'Wake Up Alone (Original Recording)'

Curtis Fuller – 'Chantized'

D'Angelo – '1000 Deaths'

Earth, Wind & Fire – 'See the Light'

Miguel – 'Where's the Fun in Forever'

Kadhja Bonet – 'Remember the Rain'

Sun-El Musician feat. Samthing Soweto – 'Akanamali'

Denai Moore – 'Does It Get Easier?'

Renée Zellweger, Catherine Zeta-Jones & Taye Diggs – 'Nowadays/Hot Honey Rag (Medley Title)'

GUKA'S HANDS, OR THE FIRST TIME MY HANDS SHOOK

I am sitting upright in bed. I have been awake for less than two minutes. I am looking at my hands and they are shaking.

I don't know why my hands are shaking.

I know why my hands are shaking.

I must be diabetic. This is a diabetic thing, right?

It is the morning on a weekday, and Mum has left me in your care. She had no other choice—she had to go to work. I don't know where Cucu, Susie or the maid are. It is strange and exciting that I've been left with you.

Or maybe I'm having a stroke. Or that tumour I'm convinced I have somewhere has grown.

We are at the dining room table and I am reaching up to cling to its surface.

And yet, even as I self-diagnose, I am calm. I am staring calmly at my hands because in the half second that it took for me to recognise that

You ask me if I'd like some tea and I say yes. I watch you as you lift the pot and pour into my mug. Your hands are shaking. 'This is my hands were shaking, I realised that this moment preceded one of my earliest memories. It came before somehow and is the reason why that memory is a memory and not one of the billions of fleeting moments that is forgotten as soon as it passes.

I know why my hands are shaking.

what happens when people get old,' I think to myself. I feel sorry for you. For some reason, I decide that this is an important truth to have learned. I decide that I will always have this memory.

I know why my hands are shaking.

INTRODUCTION

The origins of this book can be traced back to my diary entries in the final two years I spent trying to get sober. These writings don't really document the deepening chaos and loneliness of addiction, but they do map out my felt sense of time during those years.

From these fragmented reflections, which range from calmly reasoned to despairing to unintelligible, addiction emerged as a temporal phenomenon, as the dangerous and bewildering architect of a new form of time to which the usual rules did not apply. A transparent bubble submerged in the stream of 'normal' time. Within the bubble was a distortion of all the laws of cause and effect, including a gradual decoupling of pain and change such that they came to exist in entirely indifferent relation to each other. And always the words 'not yet', whispered over and over like a dull, stultifying heartbeat.

Rather unimaginatively, I've come to call this time the it's-not-time. It's-not-time as in you'll have to stop soon ... but not yet. No explanation or deadline offered, just the perpetual wait for something to finally shift. But also it's-not-time as in not time as I'd ever known it before, raised as I was to understand time in terms of linear progression, history and a stable sense of the future—none of which meaningfully existed in the it's-not-time.

I could see normal time flowing around me, but it couldn't touch me. I wrote about this tension between time as I knew it should be and time as I was experiencing it. Questioned how to pierce the walls of addiction's bubble and return to normal time before I lost too much. Wondered at how it could be so ungovernable while simultaneously adhering to its own strict logic. I was intensely curious about my addiction even as it started to kill me.

I see the it's-not-time as a form of crip time, which is a concept developed by disabled people to describe the different ways we experience and relate to time and space. Like Robert McRuer, I use the word 'crip' as 'a marker of an in-your-face, or out-and-proud, cultural model of disability', which recognises disability as a valuable positionality even as it might also entail coming up against social and embodied obstacles.[1] Crip time is a reorientation to time from this political standpoint.

It exists alongside and in opposition to 'straight time', which I partially allude to above when mentioning 'normal time'. Straight time refers to an organisation of the world and human life according to straight, heteronormative timelines. These include directives to be a compliant worker, to accumulate wealth, to reproduce oneself within the heterosexual nuclear family and to do all the above within societally set time frames. Under a capitalist temporal and spatial regime, conformity to the measures of straight time is a constitutive condition of humanity itself. As Jack Halberstam writes, from the fields of psychoanalysis to medicine to socioeconomic policy, norma-tive conceptions of time outline the shape of a life worth living.[2] Inhabiting crip time entails a divestment, whether intentional or not, from straight time and its attendant pressures. The promise of this divestment when consciously chosen and criti-cally engaged with is an opening of the imagination to the very real possibilities of a less ableist, less profit-driven society and to new definitions of what it means to be human.

My mapping of addiction's crip time, along with the prin-ciples of the addict-led mutual aid recovery community that went on to save my life, has convinced me of the existence of an addict epistemology, that is, a theory of what we know and how we know that is specifically rooted in the experience of addicts. Not only are the knowledge practices that addicts develop in active addiction and recovery useful for saving our own lives;

they also add a specific and valuable lens to humanity's kaleido-scopic understanding of itself and of the world.

The purpose of this book is specifically to explore contribu-tions that an addict epistemology can make to leftist thinking. Addicts are often objectified as the passive beneficiaries of liberatory theory and action. I want to argue that we can and do contribute our own intellectual labour to liberation. One obvious example can be seen in the addict-led harm-reduc-tion initiatives in cities across the world that offer services like needle exchanges and safe consumption sites, ensuring that drug users can use safely and with dignity.

Key to the addict epistemology is that it highlights that we exist outside the boundaries and definitions offered by the medical model, which reduces addiction to individual pathology; the two-dimensional social model, which reduces addiction entirely to a process of social disablement; and the particularly stigmatising argument that addiction is nothing more than a sort of moral degeneracy or deficit in willpower. All these models promise little more than death or immiser-ation for addicts under present conditions, yet here so many of us are, alive and thriving and loving and giving and saving as many of us as we possibly can. I happily refer to myself as an alcoholic/addict, with all the stigma that carries, in part because I believe in making a claim to dignity under all condi-tions and gazes, but also because addict knowledges have shown me that I'm more than the stigma would have me believe I am.

I'm not just talking about combatting stereotypes here. Addict livingness (if I can borrow a little from Katherine McKittrick) spills outside of the boxes people try and force us into and beckons a new world.[3] Addiction's urgency—its chaos and ungovernability—sets out clear demands for this new world. It tells us that access to care should not be tied to conditions such as a performance of wellness or recovery on the terms of the state. It asserts that time should be made for the it's-not-time in the form of material support—food and housing—throughout both active addiction and recovery.

To me, an unembodied addict epistemology would be extremely limited, as the most interesting insights come from addiction as a lived experience. In this book I start from my personal experience as a member of an abstinence-based recovery community and extrapolate from there. I obviously don't speak for the entire addict experience, only my own. There are as many lived experiences of addiction as there are people struggling with their substance use, and I hope those with different experiences take this book as an invitation to lend their voice, too, to the collective collation of addict knowledges.

MEMORY FAILURES

Blackout is a form of space-time travel that steals and distorts memories, and by the final years of my drinking it was happening almost daily. As a result, I've had to reshape my relationship to memory, particularly considering its ties to relation and identity. Early recovery was fraught as I questioned how I could have an accurate sense of who I was when I could barely remember some of the most formative years of my life. What did it mean for my friendships and other relationships that I couldn't recall any of the work that I'd put into making or keeping them?

As always, the solution lay in community, specifically my recovery community. There, a woman told me she had lost a whole decade, a period when she had got married and had both of her children, very little of which she could remember. Her calm, almost nonchalant tone, along with the ease and grace with which she carried herself, suggested to me that ultimately identity and relation must rely on more than just memory; they must be more than some positivist project of stacking up successive recollections and in that way building a sense of self and of others.

In any case, as my first sponsor reminded me, everyone— addict or otherwise—forgets most of their life, and very little of what anyone does remember is recalled as it actually happened. We're all engaged in the farce of imbuing memory with more certainty than it can really offer us. Blackout just brings this fact home more strongly for some of us.

Accepting some of that uncertainty, I'm now more interested

in trying to engage with memories on their own terms. To sit with them as they present themselves to me rather than trying to build a specific narrative. I don't do this in an effort to attain some purer truth. It has simply been the result of letting go of the fantasies about memory that I used to have.

This is what I tried to do in 'Guka's Hands' at the start of this book. It's an attempt to record a memory that rejects the form of linear narrative. As the image of my grandfather pouring me tea appeared to me that morning, it was both an old memory and a new realisation. Before the morning when my hands first shook, on the rare occasions when this memory would spring to mind, the story it told me was about the changes our bodies go through as we age, visualised from the perspective of a five-year-old with no awareness of withdrawal.

But when my own hands shook one morning almost two decades later, that memory, which hadn't presented itself for years, in half a second knitted itself together with everything else I had learned since that breakfast with my Guka. I knew instantly that my hands were shaking because of withdrawal, and the meaning of the memory changed forever. The story it captured was not about aging (after all, he can't have been older than fifty-something at the time) but about family legacies of addiction and grief, and how my Guka could still speak to me even though he died years ago.

My memory being what it is, I can't remember what event finally triggered me to get help with my drinking for the first time. There are two or three candidates from around that time, all of which feel equally true. This is one of them.

That first attempt at recording the memory feels like a failure, which I'm okay with. Using words to accurately describe memory strikes me as a losing battle. It would be easier if I were a composer or a painter and could layer different moments and affects on top of each other such that they appeared simultaneously or at least danced with and around each other more freely.

A second written attempt might follow the rules of the time-bending syntax imagined by Ted Chiang in his 1998 sci-fi short story 'Story of Your Life', which was adapted into the film *Arrival,* starring Amy Adams. In the story, a linguist, Dr Louise Banks, is tasked with translating the language of an alien species—the heptapods—who arrive on Earth with unclear intentions. Through analysing their language, which follows no linear sequence and has no reference to a spoken language, and in which every ideogram in a phrase or sentence is produced simultaneously, Louise discovers that the heptapods experience time in a way that is radically different to the way that humans do. Instead of seeing events sequentially, that is, in terms of cause and effect, they experience events all at once.

This is reflected in the heptapods' language. They already know everything that will happen, and so rather than restricting themselves to expressing ideas using one word after another, and given that they already know how each sentence will end before they start, they present every component of written dialogue concurrently. In *Arrival*, the phrases in this language appear as circles, some closed, some open, each formed of several different ideograms, which appear as thickenings of or offshoots from parts of these circles.

This idea of a beginning and an end being written simultaneously to create the meaning of both speaks to me, although one change would have to made. The heptapods, with their ability to experience all of time all at once, raise interesting questions about determinism: if everything is already known, then surely nothing can be changed. I don't buy into that.

So, if I were to write this memory as inspired by the heptapods, none of the loops could be closed. I might have the five-year-old's narrative start at one point and curve to the left while the twenty-two-year-old's perspective would start at the same point and curve to the right, yet with no point at which they would meet. I don't know yet that this memory is done with me. Whether it's given me everything that it has to give. And I don't believe that any future events that might give it new meaning are pre-determined.

The visual I imagine this time seems a lot more satisfying than my first attempt to capture the memory. It gets closer to what the memory feels like.

A final attempt might draw from sci-fi again, this time Ursula K. Le Guin's 1985 novel *Always Coming Home*. It presents a pseudo-anthropological study of the fictional Kesh people, a cultural group who live in a distant post-apocalyptic future set in what is currently known as northern California. They sing songs using something called 'matrix words', repeated syllables that are chanted by groups of singers. Each refrain is given as long as an hour before the next matrix word in the song is chanted, each chant given its space before being followed by the next.

There's something about this giving of space to each matrix word that signals that each exists in its own separate time. To me, this means that even though the song is sung sequentially, each matrix word's time could technically co-exist with the time of the next one, or of the one after that. The words do not defer to each other but are subjected to human forms of time only to the extent that we sing them. They are rarely if ever written down, as they become unintelligible if crystallised into our time so concretely; in fact, their meaning becomes miscarried in written text. According to one of the Kesh, 'writing down matrix words makes about as much sense as writing down dance-steps'.[1]

If I were to make my own matrix words, there'd be one to speak to childhood ('hayee xho'), one to a grandfather's timeless love ('ou'), one to the hiding of something for safe-keeping ('shen-shen'), one to an ancestor's ability to speak with a new kind of clarity in death ('ou-a ya'), and one to revelation ('ye'). So:

hayee xho
ou
shen-shen
ou-a ya
ye

This attempt is probably the least satisfying. For starters, it's cheating. Matrix words derive their truest meaning from the musicality of song and the breath of singers. Writing them without that context fails to solve the problem of recording memory in a non-linear format unless 1 ask the reader to assume a meaningful musical accompaniment. Again, it needs a composer.

Perhaps this is a challenge that writers must cede to other artists. Or if it simply needs a better writer, maybe a poet, 1 cede to them.

SOBER FAILURES

There are many oft-repeated sayings in my recovery community. In separate recovery meetings, I have heard the following three:

1. It takes one year to get your marbles back and another four to learn how to play with them.
2. It takes five years to get your marbles back and five to learn how to play with them.
3. It takes ten years to get your marbles back and the rest of your life to learn how to play with them.

In one sense, sober time is about re-entering the slipstream of straight time. Having occupied the spherical Groundhog Day of the it's-not-time for however long, you suddenly find in recovery that valences like 'straight' and 'up' become possible to maintain consistently, at least in theory.

This is one of the ways in which sober time is measured. People often talk about how they get to 'grow up' in recovery, usually meaning that they become able to do things like turn up to work on time or provide for a family—the most basic markers of a commitment to straight time. These accomplishments are used to mark progress, but they're also only part of the story. There are some who earn less money sober than they did drunk, others who never recover the families they lost during active addiction, or who in fact lose them *after* they get sober. Being able to cope healthily with these ostensible defeats also constitutes progress in recovery, because the most important developmental markers in sober time relate to psycho-emotional health. As long as that health is maintained, sober time is inhabited successfully.

But as the three different aphorisms above suggest, even this approach is ambiguous.

Because of our focus on life-long abstinence, time comes up a lot in meetings, and sober time in and of itself is used as a means of communicating something about a person's psycho-emotional state. Someone with one year (sober) is understood to be resilient, miraculous and probably a little unstable. A person with five or six years takes their recovery seriously and is settling in for the long haul. Anyone with ten years (at least to those with only a handful of years) automatically enters the category of 'old-timer' and is wise by default, while those with thirty-plus years are reflexively endowed with an awe-inspiring humility. Each stereotype carries differing degrees of the ultimate desired archetype of recovery: a quieter, kinder head and the ability to accept life on its own terms.

There is an undercurrent of straight-time logic to these assumptions. Across nations and cultures, whether someone is twenty-one years old, fifty years old or seven years old intrinsically tells us something about them. Age allows us to infer what stages in life a person is passing through, what their interests, desires and greatest fears are, or should be, and where they might be going next, all before we know anything else about them.

Yet while sober time draws from straight time's logic, it also disrupts it. We have our archetypes of recovery, but there is little expectation that a person actually reach them. This is what I learn from the sayings above. I heard the first from someone with just under five years of sobriety, the second a few weeks later from someone approaching ten years, and the last most recently from someone with roughly twenty years. My interpretation of the adages is that there are stages in the improvement of my psycho-emotional health that I can expect to pass through over the course of specified periods of time. And while it's up to me to define what it is to 'get my marbles back' and to 'learn how to play with them', I can get a sense of what I might want those things to mean based on how other members of the recovery community define good mental health.

But the goalposts shift constantly. I've encountered a variety of opinions of what the milestones of recovery should look like, with different goals and different time periods. Like my first sponsor suggesting I not date for the first year of sobriety, while my second sponsor said it was actually safer to wait four years (I ignored them both). Competing ideas about when one will have attained an amorphous sense of 'sanity' or the requisite presence of mind to be considered one thing or another abound, suggesting that these archetypes might be useful to work towards but that they're ultimately not the point.

Failure is the point. We can have ideas about what the product of five years of work in a recovery programme should ideally look like, but ultimately, these ideals are not attainable. You can aim to incarnate an archetype knowing all the while that it will elude you but aiming towards it anyway because it's an archetype worth failing towards. And not only is this failure expected—it's public and shared. I learned that I was expected to fail from people in recovery meetings with more time than me who opened up honestly about their own recovery. The promise of failure allows me to wear recovery loosely rather than be caged by it; the flexibility of failure is what makes my recovery sustainable.

This is not how straight time works. There, everyone is expected to actually embody whatever archetype has been socially constructed for their age group. Even as children, we are told that there is a right way to act our age, and the further we deviate, the greater the social consequences. This could mean being pathologised (an inability to keep up or fit in at school, for example, is immediately read as a problem with the child and not with the excessively restrictive nature of schooling), but it also includes punishments like bullying and social exclusion, or simply being made to feel like one is failing unduly at life, with all the pain and despair that these experiences can produce and that can follow us around all our lives.

Whatever the expectations of people in straight time, its archetypal ideals are just as impossible to meet as those of sober time. The inevitable result is that uncritically occupying straight time fosters a state of perpetual anxiety. Because each person knows deep down that they do not and may never embody their assigned archetype but feels obliged to pretend they do because they imagine everyone else is successfully being the real deal. They must love their job and be good at it, have the perfect romantic relationship, have a tight-knit friendship group, occupy their positions in their family (parent, child, aunt, grandparent) in flawless accordance with strict criteria and rules, have the correct hobbies (and monetise them wherever possible), consume the right commodities and services, perform gender in the right way ... the list goes on.

Of course, there is room for *some* failure. Increasingly, it's acceptable to confess the difficulties experienced on the way to achieving success. We can list the job rejections we received before we got onto our dream career path. Modern heterosexuality is rife with talk of just how much work marriage is. Mothers get to be honest about how tiring child-rearing in the nuclear family can be.

TV comedies like *Fleabag* and *Motherland* emerge as means for us to safely project anxieties about our own failures and our suspicions that the archetypal ideals are out of our reach onto others. Part of what makes these shows great art is that they serve this essential social function, reminding us that we're allowed to break from time to time because other people do. They are political to the extent that they expose the structures, such as patriarchy, that foist such impossible archetypes upon us in the first place. They reveal these archetypes to be often contradictory.

But discussing failure and embracing it are two different things. In fact, the notion of failing and trying again is itself folded into many of the elusive archetypes, yet it is with the understanding that failures are only acceptable when they are part of the journey to success. The expectation of success can seem positive and uplifting, until one considers that even the successes of those who do appear to fulfil an archetypal ideal often depend on the failures of those who don't. One classic example is the woman who 'has it all'—a family and a career—who is usually dependent for the care of her children and household on the labour of other women. These women in turn are not expected to ever embody such an archetype and are consistently punished for that failure, labelled too lazy, unintelligent or otherwise undeserving to garner similar success.

Instead of attempting to do away with the very concept of social archetypes, sober time presents an alternative way of engaging with them. Its first step is developing ideals that are tied to well-being as opposed to capitalist demands; it then cultivates these in a space of knowing that we can fail in working towards what we want and still continue to try. This creates time for humanity in all its freed and variegated forms, a flourishing of different kinds of lives and desires.

Sanity as the point of no return

Failure is baked into the three sayings at the start of this piece in two other ways. The first is the implication in the concept of getting your marbles 'back' that a former state of sanity existed that can be recovered. That there was once a time when you had your marbles and then lost them, a time to which you can theoretically return.

Within the context of a recovery community in which many people see the core of addiction not as something born of chaotic drug usage but as a life-long psycho-emotional disturbance that has been treated with drugs, it's obvious that there is no lost point of sanity to try to get back. The time that preceded addiction was also an undesirable period of untreated mental illness. That these maxims came out of this community anyway suggests again that failure is the point. Whatever ideal might be conjured in our minds when we think of sanity is ersatz. Even if someone felt they were pretty well adjusted before their addiction, any ideal of sanity that they might hold would still be informed by socially constructed archetypes that are both punishing and impossible to attain. These archetypes often fail to account for all the ways the world can negatively impact our mental health. They ignore how circumstances of exploitation and precarity are likely to induce anxiety, low mood or a whole host of other mental health issues for which someone might self-medicate with alcohol or other drugs. They demand that the individual sort out their head and then return to the same unhealthy conditions without falling ill again. In this context, the ultimate value of the marbles metaphor is in its potential to encourage us to construct a new conception of psycho-emotional health for ourselves—one that feels fulfilling and worth failing towards.

Failure is built into the very notion of 'recovery', which derives etymologically from the Latin *recuperare*, meaning 'get back' or 'get again'. Where sanity is a socially constructed myth or where what came before addiction was itself undesirable, recovery always entails failure. This is precisely why I like the word, and why I continue to use it. It reminds me that failure is the point. When I say 'recovery', I don't imagine a phenomenon governed by some linear conception of time, an image of diversion and return. Instead, I picture the tide tirelessly reaching out to the shore and pulling away again. Unceasing and timeless.

Within the ludic quality of the sayings there is also failure. Play connotes childlikeness, an unwillingness to grow up even as we are able to attain some of the grown-up markers of straight time. Play is open-ended, done on one's own terms, imaginative, freeing. It is utterly disruptive. Contrary to a sanist interpretation of what it would mean to get one's marbles back, the sayings encourage us to engage with our minds playfully, an attitude that highlights that the purpose of getting sober is not to then be coerced into mimicking a form of consciousness constructed by the status quo. We don't develop better psycho-emotional health to better slot into society. We do it for ourselves, and it is only a beginning.

So, what might sober failures have to do with people not in recovery? Perhaps they offer suggestions for how collective life could be made.

Failure is already a leftist rubric developed in opposition to late-capitalist norms. Jack Halberstam, in *The Queer Art of Failure*, outlines an argument for failure as presenting an opportunity to live differently. For Halberstam, success under heteronormative, capitalist conditions 'equates too easily to specific forms of reproductive maturity combined with wealth accumulation'.[1] He sees the potential of failure to allow us to escape punishing, disciplining social norms by embracing the 'wondrous anarchy of childhood' and allowing the negative affects of failure like disillusionment and despair to 'poke holes in the toxic positivity of contemporary life'.[2]

Thus, failure is already being used in the process of building a new world. Sober failure as a specific affect might speak to what comes after capitalism, when failure as a stance against capitalism is no longer as intelligible or as urgent. While I see the future as something unknowable towards which we gesture rather than concretely plan, I think it's useful to consider the role of new archetypes for political organising and being, and how we can construct them outside the coercive logics of straight time. What might it mean to construct positive archetypes worth failing towards, towards which we fail together? What space for humanity and diversity might that create? How might that affect what archetypes we choose to construct, if they're to be worn as a loose garment and not to be a restrictive cage?

The notion of not returning is also something that could relate to political life, to the extent that one thinks in terms of counter-revolution or Marxist teleology. But play is even more important. Revolution, like recovery, is as much about seizing pleasure as it is about eradicating misery. To gain freedom and justice and learn how to play with them seems to me a joyful end-goal.

Forgetting

Partially by virtue of our renewed participation in straight time, it's inevitable that addicts forget the benefits of partici-pating in sober time and its failures. Straight time's propaganda hits us just as hard as it does others, if not even harder, given the feeling of having wasted time in active addiction. Years into sober time, I'm still fighting the instinct that I need to catch up with peers who haven't been slowed down by illness, and I hear people who got sober later in life bemoan wasted decades.

So much of recovery work, then, is collective remembering. Getting sober might allow us to participate in straight time, but we can't let it trick us into forgetting how to be outside it.

The easiest way to prevent forgetting is repetition, hence the constant repetition of aphorisms like the ones at the start of this piece, making a full circle between sober time and the it's-not-time. In active addiction, repetition is rife and often read as a sign of stupidity. An inability to break out of the time loop created when each day is shaped by the substance of choice. Needing to have things repeated to us over and over because we are not fully present or in a position to lucidly receive information. Speaking repetitively ourselves. I frequently found myself initiating the same conversations again verbatim, only realising I'd done so when it was pointed out or when a specific and increasingly familiar look of confusion passed over people's faces.

In recovery, the rhythm of this litany of oblivion is retooled in service of improved wellbeing. Halberstam writes about how stupidity and forgetfulness can 'work hand in hand to open up new and different ways of being in relation to time, truth, being, living, and dying'.[3] The practice of repetition is adopted again in recovery, not as a sign of forgetting but as an act of remembering and in service of living. Received wisdom is repeated over and over as a collective reminder after our individual adventures in straight time that we belong to sober time. Not just in meetings but in conversations with sponsors and catch-ups with friends. We draw tactics from the old place of unknowing in active addiction to help craft a new way of knowing in recovery.

This goes right down to the level of continuing to call myself an alcoholic after a few years of sobriety and repeating that I am one several times a week in meetings. There's an anxiety this sparks in people who have never struggled with their substance use (and in many people who have), and I suspect this anxiety is caused by a cultural obsession with cure.

In *Brilliant Imperfection: Grappling with Cure*, Eli Clare writes that dominant narratives surrounding cure associate it with restoration from a damaged state of being to a prior, better state.[4] Lisa Fannen adds in *Warp & Weft* that this ideology fails to honour the potentially important transformations that one can undergo in illness or disability.[5] Rather than a valuable ontological position, illness is generally seen as an interruption to 'normal' life to be overcome, and then, ideally, forgotten. Conceding to disability as a perpetual state can therefore be seen as a moral failing, particularly where addiction is concerned, given that even those who know to call it an illness rarely actually see it as one.

Yet I have absolutely no desire to go back, to be restored. I do not want to recover my state of mind before I discovered alcohol, when I endlessly craved the infinite and had no way of accessing it. Only through active addiction have I come to a place where I can mitigate that craving and find meaning within it. My personal conception of failure, failure as a purely negative and futile valence, would be reversion to the person I was before I was changed by addiction.

The label 'alcoholic' also has the potential to bend time and memory. For me, the most dangerous form of forgetting in active addiction was forgetting that I'm an alcoholic (or at the very least forgetting the consequences of my alcoholism), something that would happen over and over. There was one particularly dark consequence of my drinking that I wanted to remember, because as it was happening I knew that if I held on to that despair I would never be able to drink again. But just two days later, I could already feel the memory beginning to fade. By the end of the week, the anguish evoked when I remembered was a hopeless reconstruction rather than the real thing. I was drunk again the next day.

Today, almost five years later, I remember it as vividly as if it happened yesterday. Emotions I couldn't access a week after the episode invade my bodymind whenever I think about it now. Recovery can distort memory just as much as addiction. My continued use of the labels 'addict' and 'alcoholic' is a way of acknowledging this, that that experience isn't something discrete that I left in the past but one that is made and unmade in the present and can be changed again in the future. Should I stop treating my alcoholism, I suspect that memory and others like it would start to fade again. I take out insurance against this whenever I choose repetition over cure.

Admittedly, this opens up a complicated conversation about the relationship between the unwillingness to forget and trauma. I might be rejecting another form of healing in welcoming the sometimes overwhelming memories of the most painful parts of active addiction. My response to this is personal: none of what I remember is so distressing as to be debilitating or to prevent me from carrying out what I believe to be a happy life. I welcome the memories because, as much as my recovery today is primarily about maximising the happiness of myself and others, it is essential that I never forget what brought me here in the first place.

Much as with blackout, in forgetting, remembering and repeating, I open myself up to the unreliability of memory. I follow it in crip directions rather than trying to turn it into a positivist tool that renders the past immutable, solid ground on which to build. I let unknowing blossom into knowing.

Inconvenient recovery

There is a final contradiction to consider, and that is how sober time simultaneously gives me the ability to participate in straight time and consistently pulls me out of it. The activities required for my recovery include praying and meditating every morning, attending hour-long meetings at least three times a week, calling alcoholics every day, regularly meeting with my sponsor and sponsees, and writing gratitude lists every night at minimum. All of these things are an inconvenience when my focus is on participating in straight time. The alarm to call another alcoholic almost always goes off mid-way through drafting an email, precious evenings and weekends are taken up by meetings, conversations with loved ones are missed out on, and even the writing of this book has been disrupted.

This is true for me even though, for the most part, I'm nowhere near as time-poor as many others are. While there are at least a hundred addiction meetings a week in London, many are organised by people who work a regular nine-to-five, which significantly limits the options of people who don't. New mothers, shift workers, night owls—all have to find a way to make recovery work while also battling the constraints of straight time. The proliferation of online meetings that were set up during the pandemic lockdowns have helped significantly, but it remains the case that part of what makes recovery hard is how inconvenient it is.

Amongst members of my recovery community, a grim pleasure can be found in this fact. It is a mark of pride to be so willing to be tired and inconvenienced. It also becomes an easy way to dismiss people when they relapse—they simply valued straight time's promises more than those of sober time.

But I don't think this inconvenience is inevitable or necessary. In the same way that active addiction's urgency calls forth a new world, so, too, does the inconvenience of recovery. If our ability to care for ourselves is hampered by straight time, then maybe there's an issue with straight time.

To divest entirely is impossible for most (we have to eat and pay rent), but I think if we inhabit straight time critically, we can also start making demands for ourselves and for all those thrown in and out of the it's-not-time, unable to ever get a consistent hold on sober time because straight time makes it virtually impossible.

IS ADDICTION
A DISABILITY?

Whether or not addiction is a disability is not, in itself, a particularly interesting or productive question. In fact, it's difficult to find an all-encompassing definition of disability in the first place. Different answers and models have arisen precisely because it's such a slippery concept. The most well known include the medical model, which identifies disability as a problem solely in the impaired body of an individual and which focuses on eliminating difference between bodyminds. Against this two-dimensional and often violent approach, the social model emerged as a way of locating disability in ableist social structures, which prevent people with bodymind impairments from being able to participate fully in society. Then there's Alison Kafer's hybrid relational model, in which disability is 'experienced in and through relationships', rendering it contingent and complex.[1]

Assuming there were one definition of disability that the majority of people could get behind, I still wouldn't be interested in making a case for addiction's inclusion. But I ask the question because I am curious to know what happens when addiction is denied the designation of a disability.

To answer this question, I look at two case studies. The first addresses the campaigning strategy of a subset of chronic pain patients in the United States, who have become unexpected casualties in the opioid crisis. The second brings us back to the United Kingdom and the Equality Act 2010, under which addiction is explicitly excluded from the legal definition of disability.

'We're patients, not addicts'

In 2016, the Centers for Disease Control and Prevention (CDC) issued prescribing guidelines for opioids in the face of a large wave of deaths from drug overdose in the USA. That year alone there were 64,000 overdose deaths across the country, 42,000 of which were attributed to opioids. The cause of this crisis was largely laid at the feet of doctors over-prescribing opioid pain medication. In its recommendations to primary-care physicians on how to treat new patients, the CDC therefore limited the number of days opioids should be prescribed for and the dosage amount.

These recommendations ended up being applied as black-letter law. State legislators set about enshrining them in statute and even expanded their ambit to apply to healthcare professionals more broadly, including specialists in the treatment of pain. The consequences for chronic pain (CP) sufferers were catastrophic. According to the Pain Advocacy Coalition, a grass-roots patient-led advocacy group, the CDC's guidelines sparked an 'opioid hysteria' that eroded the patient–physician–pharmacist relationship and marginalised an entire class of patients. Human Rights Watch documented some of the resulting abuses, which included social isolation, suicidal ideation and self-medication with the use of alcohol or illicit drugs.[2]

The CDC has since acknowledged that the sweeping policy decisions that emerged as a result of the 2016 guidelines were misguided, and at the end of 2022 it released updated prescribing recommendations. This was in part due to the work of CP activists who had been organising for their right to life-saving and -improving pain treatment since the publication of the original guidelines. A subset of these organisers sought to turn media focus away from patients with CP and towards the real subjects of the opioid crisis: addicts. Taglines such as 'we're patients, not addicts' began to materialise during protests and in online campaigns. The rationale was that responsible patients being treated for pain with opioid medication were being wrongly conflated with addicts, whose use of heroin and illicit fentanyl was the actual cause of the overdose epidemic. More compassionate activists conceded that addicts deserved care while maintaining that their needs should not interfere with the ability of people diagnosed with CP to access the medication they needed. In short, these were not people trying to score—they were rational patients with healthcare needs, and they deserved to be treated as such.

This wasn't a surprising strategy given that media narratives have in fact conflated CP sufferers with addicts as part of a wider misunderstanding of the nature of both CP and addiction. It is, however, a troubling one.

For starters, the CP activists' line of argument reinforces the stigma of addiction. The clear implication is that patients are people who deserve care from medical institutions whereas addicts are not, or at the very least that the waters are muddied where addicts are concerned. The general class of patienthood is claimed for some, CP sufferers, and presented as directly opposing and excluding others, addicts. If the argument were simply that CP sufferers and addicts are two separate categories of patients (which, in itself, is not always true) who need different approaches to their care, then the tagline 'patients, not addicts' would make no sense; something more specific like 'pain patients, not addicts' would be more appropriate. Instead, what's being argued is that CP sufferers belong to a pre-existing category of people deserving of medical care—patients—while addicts do not.

In *The War on Drugs and the Global Colour Line*, Kojo Koram succinctly describes how the social construction of 'drugs' has facilitated the social construction of the 'addict'.[3] Within a capitalist, post-Enlightenment context that defines the rational man in part by his capacity for delayed gratification and his ability to reason in specific ways, drugs appear as transgressive substances—ones that control otherwise rational consumers and distort free-market laws of demand. Therein lies the root of the stigma that surrounds drug users, healthy or otherwise, who are deemed to abandon these traits of the rational man and to that extent give up their claim to humanity.

Addicts embody this inhumanity as people who don't just dabble with this loss of control but whose lives are centred around it. Part of what underpins the subhumanity of addicts is our incapacity to reason. The inability to make the rational decision to stop using drugs in the face of overwhelming negative consequences is seen as a reflection of a general incapacity to make rational decisions about anything. It is assumed there is something fundamentally wrong with us that renders us incapable of being trusted with ourselves or with anything of value. This imagined state of mind is antithetical to the ideal Enlightenment figure, who has total control over not only his mind but also his environment.

It seems that the argument being made with the line 'patients, not addicts' is that CP sufferers should be returned to the archetype of the ideal Enlightenment figure—an archetype of which 'patient' is assumed to form part—rather than be lumped in with addicts, who could not have the sort of patient–physician relationship that these activists desire. CP sufferers will then be able to engage with their doctors from this recognised position of rationality again and gain access to the care they deserve. The explicit invocation of addicts as a point of contrast illustrates that, much like the rational Enlightenment figure, who could only be invented in opposition to the racialised savage, the figure of the patient cannot exist independently and relies on an abject relation to a subhuman object in order to be legible.

Addicts are presented not only as wholly oppositional to patients but as in need of expulsion, since we threaten both their bodily integrity and what it means to be a patient altogether. Where the two categories collide (as in the case of CP sufferers), the addict emerges as the more powerful identifier, materially impacting the ability of those who identify as patients to get the healthcare they would otherwise be entitled to by virtue of being patients. Any association with addicts must therefore be vehemently rejected. The patient is rational *because* they eject the irrational addict other. The patient cannot exist without the addict. This is the purpose that the addict serves in this framing; this is what is achieved by the removal of the addict from the category of illness/disability.

The consequences of this kind of framing are material. Addicts and CP sufferers alike have been denied medical treatment and threatened with criminal arrest on the basis of what is, or is deemed to be, drug-seeking behaviour. Take Ken Adams, a man who was struggling with a painful and at the time undiagnosed abdominal adhesion issue. After more than twenty trips to seek help at the emergency room over one and a half years, on his final visit Adams was outright refused care because he asked directly for the powerful opioid that would treat his condition without first waiting to see if standard morphine would work. Instead of being viewed as an example of patient knowledge about what they need, this was classed as drug-seeking behaviour, and Adams was kicked out of the hospital and threatened with arrest.[4]

Rather than recognise that such cruel and carceral reactions to anyone trying to access drugs, whether they're suffering from pain or addiction, constitute gross medical negligence, proponents of 'patients, not addicts' framing simply seek to ensure that they are never confused for addicts, for whom such a response would presumably be appropriate. Never mind that a person seeking drugs as the result of a compulsion outside of their control or simply to cope with difficult life conditions should also be met with care. Or indeed that seeking medical supply is arguably a 'rational' response to addiction, given how unsafe illicit drug supply can be. The perennial solution for dealing with addicts is punishment, just as the solution to any harmful drug use is coercion, often through the enforcement of abstinence-based recovery programmes.

The repercussions of this framing extend beyond withholding care from addicts. As constructed by the status quo, we're simply an embodiment of unreasoned disorder, a state of mind that can be projected onto anyone else excluded from the Enlightenment ideal so as to justify discrimination against them.

Under this logic, people of colour, already largely denied access to liberal subjecthood under the wider project of white supremacy, are at perpetual risk of being kept outside the category of patient, particularly when we do not or cannot perform conformity with racist ideals around the rational patient. When we also consider that black people are constructed not only as irrational but also as presumptive users and purveyors of illicit drugs (if not as addicts) as part of the ongoing global war on drugs, we start to see how dangerous this framing really is. Illicit drug consumption and possession, implied and actual, are already used as a justification for state violence against black people; it's not a stretch to say that they might also be used to legitimise the withholding of care. How can we trust medical professionals operating in this context to consistently believe black people who make claims to patienthood?

Similar arguments can be applied to women, who are still too often disbelieved or dismissed by doctors when seeking care, particularly where pain is concerned. Or to refugees and asylum seekers, who are more likely to be portrayed as drains on the healthcare system than as patients and who face the risk of meeting a border instead of a carer when they seek medical attention.

With this in mind, I'm not convinced that CP sufferers in general, once delivered from their association with addicts, will really be able to occupy the position of rational patients and be treated as rational equals by their doctors. After all, disabled people have also long been deemed abject within the Enlightenment's political project, a fact that civil rights activists have been working to undercut for years. The Pain Advocacy Coalition's motto, 'it's not a conversation about us, without us,' is evocative of the call of many disabled civil rights organisers. Civil rights discourse relies on the reproduction of liberal subjecthood, whether applying it to the person making a claim to rights or in an appeal to the 'civilised' society's responsibility to care for those who cannot care for themselves. One could argue that the efforts of disabled activists within the liberal model of civil rights have been to reposition themselves from being 'objects to be cared for' to being 'subjects with rights'. This is both because they *are* subjects and because wider society's attempts to 'care' for them have largely produced the opposite effect.

But how successful can this shift be when the entire project of liberal subjecthood is antithetical to notions of interdependence that are often at the core of disabled experience? When the rational man should be dependent on no one but himself and be able to provide labour power continually and at the least possible cost to his employer? And when sanist conceptions of rationality are deemed superior to the ways that neurodivergent people and people with intellectual or developmental disabilities think and reason? This isn't even to touch upon the structural obstacles that prevent most disabled people from being able to protect their rights because they lack fair access to legal advice or representation.

Moreover, in spite of the work that many organisers have done to bring dignity to the category of the patient, it is still frequently used as a place to throw away society's undesirables. People who are unproductive or resistant to the violence of capitalism can be pathologised—labelled as 'patients'—and consequently shut away in institutions or otherwise segregated from the rest of the population/workforce. The positionality of the patient remains deeply complicated, and relying on an idealised conception of patienthood as a path to freedom is a plan likely doomed to fail.

Even if unconvinced that addicts and other chaotic drug users deserve care, these CP activists are still left with the fact that the line they try to draw between patients and addicts is nowhere near as clear as they would like it to be. Some CP patients are addicts (whether or not this has anything to do with the drugs they were prescribed). The patients versus addicts framing also erases CP sufferers who engage in 'addict' practices, like procuring illicit pain medication or otherwise self-medicating in response to the gatekeeping of medical professionals.

Coalitional ties make more sense, as does divesting from the notion that the ability to behave 'rationally' should be a precondition to being heard by a doctor. In *Letter to a Young Doctor,* Johanna Hedva names the one moment when they felt part of a relationship of mutual trust and respect with a psychiatrist during an in-patient stay at a German hospital. Hedva had a panic attack one afternoon, triggered by the fact that they couldn't remember how Vincent van Gogh had committed suicide ('a story I know by heart, so forgetting it alarmed me'). Rather than restrain or dismiss them, the doctor connected with them, telling them about a Van Gogh exhibition he had recently visited, how he was 'surprised at how small the canvasses are, just this big, and how yellow and vibrant the suns and flowers are'. He spoke in this way until language finally returned to Hedva.[5]

This anecdote also speaks to the potential of healthcare without gatekeeping or unequal power dynamics. One where those seeking care do not have to perform rationality but are met where they are, as they are, and respected all the same. That these moments of care in healthcare are so rare reminds me of why the peer-to-peer work that lies at the heart of many recovery programmes is so important—addicts treating other addicts, with or without support from the state. When addicts are already practising radical approaches to healthcare, creating a dichotomy between patients and addicts only obscures this potential. It seems obvious that instead of separating ourselves from each other, we should be working together in solidarity against ableist medical norms and structures, trying to realise a more caring future for us all.

'Not amounting to an impairment'

I now turn to the UK to explore another context in which addicts are explicitly denied a designation that grants access to certain protections: 'disability' as defined by the Equality Act 2010. The Act brought together over 100 separate pieces of equality legislation, including the Disability Discrimination Act 1995, which made it illegal for the first time for employers to discriminate against disabled people.

Under Section 6 of the Equality Act 2010, disability is defined as a 'physical or mental impairment' that has a 'substantial' and 'long-term' (lasting twelve months or more) negative effect on one's ability to carry out normal daily activities. Guidance on the Act states that the word 'impairment' should be given 'its ordinary meaning' and that it would not be possible to provide an exhaustive list of conditions that qualify. A broad range of examples is offered nonetheless, including mental health conditions such as depression and anxiety disorders.[6]

Active addiction could fall under this definition, being a mental health condition with the potential to be long-term and that has a substantial adverse effect on many people's ability to carry out day-to-day tasks. Yet it is expressly excluded from the scope of the legislation under the Equality Act 2010 (Disability) Regulations 2010, which states that addiction is to be treated as 'not amounting to an impairment'. The sole exception to the exclusion is where the addiction 'was originally the result of the administration of medically prescribed drugs or other medical treatment'. In this way, people struggling with substance use are removed from the protection of the law—if they have less than two years' continuous employment, a person can be fired for their addiction, regardless of whether it's impacting their job performance. The mere threat of becoming a less efficient worker is sufficient.

To understand exactly what is being done here, we have to return again to the nebulous task of defining disability. The

Act definitively follows a medical model, focusing entirely on the body of the disabled individual as something that must be accommodated to become part of the workforce, with no recognition of the ways that disability is socially produced. Another of the medical model's basic assumptions taken up by the Act is that, in the absence of treatment, disability is something that is outside of an individual's control. The exclusion of addiction from the Act's medical-legal definition of disability then suggests both that an addicted body cannot or should not be incorporated into the workplace, and that addiction is a choice and therefore not a disability.

This view of choice is confirmed by the fact that addictions arising from medical treatment are exempt from the exclusion, the implication being that such individuals did not choose to be prescribed addictive medication and to become impaired. An addiction that develops from participation in, for example, a methadone programme could also qualify as a legal disability, as this signals that a correct choice has been made to move along the state's path to recovery and away from addiction.

There is no logical reason to distinguish between the causes of an addiction to determine whether it constitutes an impairment—unless, of course, the point is actually to penalise certain kinds of behaviour. At its core, the exclusion of addicts from the Act's protection serves a disciplining function, punishing the use of socially acceptable drugs like alcohol to excess or of illicit drugs at all.

The notion of disability as non-choice slots neatly into the liberal discourse of civil rights described above, which commonly puts forward the argument that it is unjust to discriminate against people for characteristics outside of their control. Staying with this logic, we see that the purpose of the Act is to protect members of marginalised groups from discrimination in their right to sell their labour power—a right which, under capitalism, is intimately tied to the ability to pay for necessities like food and housing and which therefore should not be unfairly suppressed.

So, what does it mean to exclude addicts from this Act, rendering their position in the workforce fundamentally precarious? On the assumption that capital acts only to ensure its own reproduction, how are capitalist ends served by limiting the pool of workers in this way?

I'll come back later to the obvious stereotype that might come to mind (that addicts make terrible workers). Let's start instead by looking at another way of defining disability, this time as a category produced by economic relations. American writer and disability rights activist Marta Russell analyses how disability 'is used to classify persons deemed less exploitable or not exploitable by the owning class who control the means of production in a capitalist economy'.[7] She explains how the creation of the disabled body, defined in this way by its non-exploitability, is in fact essential to the process of capitalism's self-perpetuation.

One of the main ways that capitalism benefits from producing disability is through the relegation of disabled people to what Marxists have termed the 'reserve army of unemployed labour'. This is a section of the working class whose labour power is rendered superfluous to capitalist exploitation as the expansion of production means that more surplus value can be derived from fewer workers. Consequently, large swathes of potential workers are condemned to what Marx termed 'enforced idleness'; regardless of their ability to work, they are unneeded.[8] The existence of this reserve army is necessary for capitalism's functioning since it provides a constant supply of easily exploitable labour that exceeds demand, weakening workers' bargaining power and enabling the owners of capital to employ and dispose of labour according to what is most profitable.

Russell's argument is that disabled workers, who cost more to employers via the provision of 'reasonable workplace adjustments' and who produce surplus value at a slower rate than non-disabled workers, make up a disproportionate portion of this reserve army. The disabled body is effectively invented in relation to the prevailing rate of labour exploitation; those unable to keep up are classed as disabled and, should they fall far enough behind, are rendered unemployed, joining the reserve army of labour that cannot be efficiently exploited by capitalists.

Beyond acting as a constant reservoir of unexploited labour, this surplus population also serves capitalist interests by maintaining compliance among workers who are in employment. For all the talk of benefit scroungers, the conditions of the reserve army are not good. If a genuine safety net existed for those not in work, then, as Russell argues, workers would be in a better position to bargain for higher wages and better working conditions. But when the only alternative to employment is a punishing, byzantine state welfare system that offers a pittance to live on, the capitalist class has an easier time controlling its workers.

And disability also serves a third function under capitalism. For the portion of the disabled population who cannot work at all and who are simply regarded as surplus, their purpose becomes to exist as a source of profit for the capitalist class. Beatrice Adler-Bolton and Artie Vierkant expound a theory of 'extractive abandonment' in their book *Health Communism*, stating that disabled people are often segregated from their communities in nursing homes or rehab centres that are increasingly becoming a focus of finance capital.[9] Many of these institutions are bled for profit at the expense of the quality of care that their 'clients' or 'customers' receive. If value cannot be extracted from our bodies as workers, then profit can be generated from the cost of our care.

The exclusion of addicts from disability under the Equality Act shines a spotlight on capitalism's reserve army and renders us its natural conscripts. Without legal protection, we can be employed when needed and discarded at will.

This isn't to say that inclusion in the legal definition of disability is a guaranteed win. Indirect discrimination against disabled workers is still lawful when justified for health and safety reasons or due to the needs of the business, while whether reasonable adjustments in the workplace are given depends on factors like the size of the business and the cost of the proposed adjustments. Then there's the sheer difficulty of bringing a successful discrimination claim. A government survey of Employment Tribunal applications found that in 2018, only 26 per cent of discrimination cases that went to a full tribunal hearing were successful. Most cases were withdrawn or dismissed before they even reached this stage.

Finally, as Marta Russell explains, the definition of disability can be changed by the ruling class in order to expand or contract the surplus class based on the needs of production. This takes us back to the legislative decision not to produce a set definition of 'impairment' in the Equality Act. While this is a reflection of the genuine ambiguity around the definition of the word, it also gives the state and its apparatus immense leeway to amend the definition of disability for economic or political reasons.

Thus, the point is not so much to argue for addiction's inclusion in the medico-legal category of disability. Rather, its exclusion leads me to argue for a world in which the ability to live a life of dignity isn't tied to the ability to be exploited. Where people aren't kept in poverty in order to increase company profits or guarantee compliance from the rest of the working population.

If we lean into stereotypes of addiction, not just that it's a choice but that it goes without saying we're useless workers, so of course it makes no sense to give us employment rights, this only cracks the imagination open wider. I resist the urge to argue that no one chooses addiction and that many addicts work for years and do so very effectively because I don't want to plead for inclusion on the government's terms, even though these statements are true and are therefore good counters to the stereotype. So what if it was a choice? So what if we're malingerers? In a less ableist world, under conditions that didn't prioritise profit above all else but instead centred the dignity of all people, neither fact would have anything to do with our ability to feed or house ourselves, to receive the care we needed from each other and from others, and to contribute to our communities in whatever ways we could manage.

The abjection of our position ushers in a new world with urgency. It pushes the imagination and forces us to ask questions about what inclusion looks like at the communist horizon. What ideas that capitalist hegemony has turned into common sense could we discard, like that those who can't or won't contribute in specific ways deserve fewer fundamental rights? What purpose will the label of disability serve post-capitalism, assuming it continues to be a useful lens through which to see the world?

I think that when addiction is denied the designation of disability, both in these case studies and in other examples, the effect is to obscure the new world. To smudge, place in shadow, distract, send our attention elsewhere, anywhere aside from the point. But to argue for addiction's inclusion in the label can also cement this obscuring by reifying normative definitions of disability and hiding the fact that disability itself is nebulous.

With that said, I do see my addiction as a disability and refer to it as such. It's through my experience with addiction that I developed my interest in disability politics. It's a personal choice, and I can offer no coherent explanation beyond that it simply feels right, and that I do so without believing that there's a set definition of disability or that it's a designation that can save me from the stigma of being an alcoholic. Consequently, my first response to the question, 'is addiction a disability?' is less 'yes', 'no,' or 'it depends'. It's usually, 'why do you ask?'

RHYTHM

I watch the rhythm of my friends' lives. Undulations in long waves punctuated by essays, occupations, heartbreak, holidays, nights out.

Normal things.

I slice diagonally across the musical phrases that make up their lives. Always out of time. Offering nothing but a choppy syncopation to dinner table conversations, from which I have to repeatedly excuse myself to down the contents of a hidden flask behind the door, because no one is drinking from their wine glasses fast enough.

The telltale thundering of my heart that tells me withdrawal has started again interrupts movies, prematurely ends a catch-up at the pub.

I come to just as the main act leaves the stage at a concert and am wasted while everyone else is in the library. They all set the beat and I can't come in when I'm supposed to.

I learn that rhythm is a form of relation and I imagine that recovery, once it comes, will be about pulling myself back into that collective rhythm.

Yet now that I'm here I see that their rhythm, while not a myth, was never the whole story.

I'm on holiday in Seville with my partner and I'm unsure if I want to continue the relationship. In an effort to suppress my doubts, I'm doomscrolling through Twitter while they lie next to me on our hotel bed doomscrolling through TikTok. I notice at some point that they're tapping their foot in rhythmic bursts, a classic ADHD stim. In noticing their body I notice my own, and I realise that I'm also stimming, to a completely different rhythm. Our ability to openly stim in each other's presence even where we're unsure of each other, to exist freely in one's own rhythms even when they're different to someone else's, this feels like a form of intimacy.

This crip asynchrony takes me back to addiction's syncopation. It occurs to me that if rhythm is relation, then maybe holding others in their different rhythms is intimacy. I start to wonder how much of the story that I told myself about my friends' collective rhythm back when I was in active addiction was true. I always felt like an outsider, but it's not like they stopped inviting me to dinners or concerts because I kept disappearing or cutting across what seemed like the natural rhythm of the night. Instead, they held me in my choppy rhythm as they experienced their own and each other's forms of asynchrony, which I was presumably too distracted to notice.

It'd be a difficult truth to accept; it's hard to think I was so seen at a point in my life when I felt so abject. But the longer I live in recovery, the more I notice the ways we all hold each other in our strange, sometimes wildly conflicting rhythms. Maybe one day I'll grow to accept it.

AMBIVALENCE

Towards a Less Fucked Up World: Sobriety and Anarchist Struggle is an early-2000s zine exploring the role of 'intoxication culture' in anarchist circles. Its author, Nick Riotfag, offers observations on what an anarchist sobriety could look like. One of these is in the form of an anecdote. While attending an environmental defence action camp for a week, organisers arranged for a sober space to be carved out and run alongside a large, booze-filled party that would be thrown to celebrate the final day of the camp. It was, by his description, the most 'comprehensive effort to address my needs [as a sober person] that had ever been made in a radical space'.[1] Yet he found the party unsatisfying. He felt quarantined, disappointed that there were so few sober people in the space, and bored by the lack of organised activities. I was struck by his ambivalence about the event. He genuinely appreciated the effort the organisers went to and the respect that was afforded to the sober space, but the night fell short of his expectations. He made some suggestions for how alternative sober spaces could be better organised, but the sense I got was that he wasn't actually sure of what, if anything, could be done to make a sober space as fun as a non-sober one.

I experience ambivalences of my own in my recovery. I've refused every offer from non-sober friends to hang out together sober because I assume they'd be bored, but I also feel resentful whenever I'm the only sober person on a night out. I leave almost every recovery community meeting in a better headspace than I was in when I entered, but still I go begrudgingly, bitter about the fact that for the rest of my life I'll have to attend at least three a week in order to not risk an alcoholic death.

And a more visceral ambivalence characterised active addiction. During that time, I recognised the necessity of my relationships for me to stay alive. I knew isolation was dangerous and that I was lucky to be surrounded by people willing and able to look after me. But I also heavily resented the care that I received. The shame of being a drunk moved through my body like a sickness of its own. I was sensitive to every shift in atmosphere that told me yet another house meeting had been held about me. Compassionate touches burned. I felt nauseated every time someone told me they were proud of me.

I thought about this while reading Eli Clare's article 'Stolen Bodies, Reclaimed Bodies: Disability and Queerness'. Critiquing disability activists who ignore 'the daily realities of [disabled] bodies' and focus excessively on the social causes of disability, Clare writes of the embodied experience of disability and the ambivalence that it produces: 'the reality of needing personal attendants to help us pee and shit (and of being at once grateful for those PAs and deeply regretting our lack of privacy); the reality of disliking the very adaptive equipment that makes our day-to-day lives possible.'[2]

Clare leaves this ambivalence unresolved and, in doing so, affirms that its purpose is to keep us from forgetting the body. The aim is not to diminish the value of society's becoming more caring, less structurally ableist. It is to remind the reader that our difficult bodies exist right alongside our efforts to bring a new world into being. Even where we create microcosms of care for ourselves upon which a non-ableist society might be modelled, disabled people aren't always going to be satisfied. Our best efforts will leave some of us grateful but still unhappy.

I'm discarding 'the body' here as quickly as I've invoked it, partly out of laziness but also because it's not the point. The argument is not about essentialist impairment versus socially constructed disability, or who will still be disabled once the world has been turned on its head. It's to recognise that this ambivalence, whatever its source, exists, and to share what it tells me.

The ambivalence of not knowing

To the extent that these ambivalences could ever be resolved, we don't currently have all the answers. Even outside the fetters crafted by death-making governments, those of us committed to disability justice don't yet have the tools to create the happiest possible lives for disabled people.

This is a fact expressed by Leah Lakshmi Piepzna-Samarasinha in *Care Work: Dreaming Disability Justice*, in which she describes an attempt to set up a 'care web' in the CCA Bay Area in the USA. The web was intended to resist a model of charity towards disability, instead being led and controlled by disabled people. Inspired by a successful short-term experiment in disabled-led care, a group of comrades planned to organise more long-term care amongst themselves to show that paying for a personal attendant was not the only means of getting disability support. Ultimately, the web was disbanded after a year amidst feelings of 'betrayal and hopelessness', as embodied and social obstacles prevented care from being effectively shared.[3]

That the web didn't meet its anticipated goals doesn't mean that those goals aren't achievable. It just means that even disabled communities are still working out the kinks around how to create alternatives to hierarchical and/or ableist forms of care. Acknowledging this is essential lest we needlessly curtail our own imaginations, wrongly assuming that all questions have been asked and answered.

The possibility that we have yet to formulate the most ground-breaking ideas for how to organise society so that disabled people have the greatest access to love and autonomy is one I find deeply exciting.

In practice, it also gives disabled people the freedom to respond to the question, 'what more do you want?' with, 'I don't know, but this isn't enough.' We are often coerced into performances of unmitigated gratitude, particularly where it's clear that people around us, disabled and non-disabled, have done their utmost to render spaces accessible. We're also expected to be all-encompassing founts of knowledge about how to fulfil our needs. But being the final arbiter of our own access requirements and always knowing what they are and how to meet them are two different things. The admission that we might not know what we want or need isn't an invitation to have solutions dictated to us or to be dismissed as 'too difficult'.

I think embracing ambivalence—being grateful for these commitments to care and also openly admitting that they're not enough—will help us make room for the interventions that *could* resolve that ambivalence. And where it isn't possible to resolve, we'll at least have the space to be honest.

Healing and contradiction

I've had to re-think my sponsorship style recently.

All of my sponsees so far have been black women. This hasn't been a deliberate choice (I've said yes to whoever has asked me), but I've found that it's been a means for me to heal from damage done by our shared recovery community, which, as much as it offers a glimpse of a new world, is very much tied to the present one.

The community is overwhelmingly white and largely unconcerned with this fact. I imagine some members would be more inclined to blame people of colour for choosing not to stay in the group than to engage in meaningful reflection about why there are so few of us here (this is starting to change, thanks to the tireless work of members of colour). It's indifferent by design to oppressive structures, which, to be honest, has never bothered me much, except to the extent that it means the community becomes enmeshed from time to time in a toxic positivity that views these structures as problems squarely in the minds of marginalised members. Racism, sexism and classism all become mere hurdles that can be overcome if one simply prays correctly and keeps their side of the street clean.

The community is also rife with sexual misconduct, for which members are rarely held accountable on the basis that they are sick people in need of compassion. Little thought is given to the vulnerable women and survivors of abuse who must somehow figure out how to stay in a community that would close ranks around those who harm them. I've heard members advocate for racists to have the right to spout their bigotry in meetings if it will somehow save them from drinking, failing to consider how people of colour can be expected to return to such spaces. I frequently find myself in meetings of largely middle-class people who, without malice or ill intent, deride the stereotype of the homeless alcoholic in such a way that I wonder if I'd come back if I happened to fall into that stereotype. Rather than acknowledge how sexual misconduct, racism and classism have a hand in marginalised members' leaving our community, what emerges is the narrative that the sole determinant of who stays and who goes is the strength of one's commitment to recovery.

And there's my own complicity in all of this as I retreat into PoC, women's and LGBT meetings—communities within the community where I can generally avoid the above, although even these aren't perfect. There's the black women's meeting where some of us had to fight for months for lip service to be paid to the inclusion of trans women and non-binary people, or the all-white women's meeting I visited once where I was met with outright hostility.

When I first joined my recovery community, my instincts told me that thinking about any of this would have to wait until after I had saved my life. I needed a few months' sobriety under my belt and to not have death at my door. In any case, when I looked at the comparable whiteness of other recovery groups, the contempt of doctors, the negligence of drug and alcohol service case workers, and the inaccessibility of rehabs for someone without recourse to public funds, it seemed there was no way of getting sober that wouldn't involve some form of racial trauma.

Biting the bullet, I picked a sponsor at random. A white woman who, amongst other things, went on to describe her racist beliefs to me every so often with the expectation that I'd soothe her or empathise with her. I stuck with her until I had eight months sober and felt safe to move on.

So, yes, sponsoring black women now is healing for me, since I feel I can offer to others what wasn't offered to me in my early days. Help them sift through the bad in our recovery community to get to what might save their life. I see this as explicitly black feminist work, a way of resolving the contradiction of healing in a space that can be constantly wounding. But there is a danger to this.

I'm back in my second year at university, slumped in an armchair in the reading room in the college library. I've spent the last four or five days organising a solidarity campaign for Michael Brown's family following the grand jury decision not to indict Darren Wilson, the police officer who killed him.

When I woke up to the news at the start of the week, I couldn't get out of bed. I missed my first lecture and had resigned myself to missing the second when a text from Yasmin came: she had a camera and a plan. The inertia left me immediately, and within minutes I was on my feet. I cycled to her college, where we quickly sketched out ideas for a photo campaign. The next few days passed by in a flurry. We travelled across campus photographing students with messages of solidarity. At one point, outside the law faculty, a white student placed a hand on my arm, looked into my eyes and said, 'I am so sorry.' I had no idea what he meant or why it was me he was apologising to when the people affected by this were thousands of miles away in Missouri. I muttered thanks and carried on. I stood and ran and leapt.

And then, it was done. The campaign was over, the money raised and sent to charities in Ferguson. Mike Brown is still dead. At that thought, the inertia returned and I collapsed into this chair in the library. I came here to catch up on the work I've ignored all week, but I can barely lift my head. I think about going to see Bennie or Maria instead given that the night is a write-off, but still I can't move. I reflect on the past week and a thought prickles at the back of my mind that perhaps organising is soothing and motivating. It's what got me out of bed. It switches off the part of me that feels because I'm so focused on action. I melt into service and don't have time to consider what it means to be black in a world where you're reminded black murder can be state-sanctioned and you're still expected to go to your morning lectures with the rest of your peers. It restores meaning to life because it feels like the only rational response to injustice. But it is so much work, and at the end of it all, those we mourn are still dead, those not brought to justice roam free.

My phone lights up with another text from Yasmin and I remember she invited me to a house party tonight. A party means alcohol. The prickling thought grows. There are other ways to not feel. Other ways to melt. And they require no work at all. Suddenly, I can move again. I pick up my mat and walk. I'm at Yasmin's door by 8 p.m., bottle in hand.

My sponsorship is poor when it becomes more about healing myself through others than about walking alongside someone else on her recovery journey. I've ignored signs that someone isn't ready yet, or over-shared, been avoidant, enabling or demanding, all to try to offer what my past self needed and will never have. That black feminist work is healing is true—there is affective and aesthetic value in it. I just have to be careful to make sure that there is more to it than that.

In the same way, there was nothing inherently wrong with coming to anti-racist organising at university as a coping mechanism, but continuing to organise primarily on that basis meant that when I found an easier coping mechanism, I lost the ability first to organise effectively and then to do so at all. Each attempt began to collapse beneath me, because why do all of this if I could just drink?

When I look through the photos from that campaign today, almost ten years on, I see someone with whom I later fell in love; I see strangers who went on to become and remain my closest friends. In short, organising brought me a community capable of holding me through nihilism and despair. Because of this community, black feminist action that I take now, which still helps me emotionally, can be more focused on looking outward, centring the needs of those with whom I want to be in solidarity, and accepting the limits of my power so that I'm not destroyed by them. As a sponsor, I will be failing in my purpose of helping others with their recovery if I'm obsessed with resolving contradictions on their behalf, not trusting that if I could find ways of carving out healthful space for myself in this recovery community, my sponsees can, too.

It's a balance I'll likely spend the rest of my life trying to strike. How to say, yes, this community can be racist, this world is racist, this will not end in our lifetime, and—untrue as it might sound—it's better for us drunks to address this with the empowering clarity of sobriety than the deadening dullness of intoxication. Addiction is a common and political cause of black death, and recovery is a weapon. It is not fair that you have been abandoned by the state and by those entrusted with your care, and yet the central fact of recovery is that you must focus first on changing yourself. True health—the health that comes in a world without borders, police, racism, misogyny, queerphobia, ableism, climate injustice—is not possible for us, but it is within our power to be as healthy as capitalism will allow us to be. We can become part of communities that enable us to choose accessing that power over nihilism, even as nihilism must be acknowledged as one natural response of many to the state of the world. Even and especially as the thought of accepting capitalism's ceiling on our health fills us with rage.

How to remind myself of all of this in saying it to others, without making that the point of why I say it to others. For my own sake as well as theirs.

A NOTE ON RELIGION

In the next three essays, I write about how my Christian faith impacts my political commitments. Originally, I planned to offer no explanation for this. In a global context in which the majority of the working class are in some way religious or spiritual, it makes less sense for religious Marxists to justify their faith and more sense for all Marxists committed to internationalism to accept they might have to engage with spiritual epistemologies. However, having written the essays, I think they'd benefit from being accompanied by some clarifying context.

Beginning with the presupposition that there is no expression of faith that isn't tied to the material conditions of its adherents, these essays are underpinned by a belief that Christian practice today is inextricable from its economic base—capitalism—and the class struggle that underlies it. This doesn't entail something as straightforward as two set categories of Christian: bourgeois and communist. It is simply a helpful framework for understanding how and why opposing visions of Christian life emerge from the same religion.

Often, Christians aligned with far-right ideologies are dismissed by other members of the religion as 'not real' Christians, or as people engaged in a project entirely separate from that of Christians committed to liberation. I find it more useful to remember that all expressions of Christian faith grow out of the same historical circumstances but some surface on the side of capital while others do not. This means I am always engaged in dialectical relationship with those Christians on the side of capital, which keeps me accountable. In the same way that it would be nonsensical to claim to be a Marxist while ignoring the actions of the bourgeoisie, I can't declare that my faith calls for me to be committed to social justice while simultaneously turning a blind eye to the oppression wrought by other Christians in the name of our God, particularly in light of the hegemonic dominance that many Christians benefit from globally. Enacting my faith as a communist necessarily requires direct opposition to these injustices, such as the overturning of the *Roe v. Wade* ruling on abortion in the USA or policies that punish migrants to Europe with a view to protecting so-called 'Christian values'.

The liberal instinct that says faith and state should not mix is absolutely correct, but when it comes to anti-capitalist praxis, this shouldn't morph into the mistaken belief that an apolitical Christianity is a 'good' Christianity. In fact, the temptation to place faith apart from politics is a betrayal of a religious tradition that has always been invested in the world as it actually exists, which, by necessity, involves its politics. If we believe that all should be fed and housed and that the stranger should be welcomed, then, given the current organisation of society, political action is required of us whether we like it or not. That could mean voting for fairer political leaders while mobilising for justice beyond party politics, protecting squatters' rights while agitating for free housing for all, volunteering at food banks while plotting how to seize the means of agricultural production, or helping migrants navigate a tough immigration system while imagining a world that doesn't criminalise migration.

None of this is to claim a monopolistic knowledge of God's will. God is not a communist, nor is God's redemptive aim for us capable of being reduced to political theory. But as a communist Christian, I recognise that it is a spiritual duty to take seriously that enduring political question: 'what is to be done?'

LONELINESS

Lying in bed, I wonder if it's possible to die of loneliness.

I've been sober for over three months but my routine has barely changed. I continue to organise my days such that I can spend hours alone in my bedroom. I'm not yet consciously aware that I'm doing this. All I know is I'm an exposed wire when I'm walking down the street. I feel naked, so being alone indoors is easier.

The only problem is it weighs on me like a heavy fog.

WEDNESDAY, 24 JULY 2019

MY BODY IS EMANATING LONELINESS SO PALPABLE IT IS
REFLECTING ITSELF OFF THE WALLS OF MY BEDROOM
AND RIGHT BACK AT ME. A SOUNDLESS CANONICAL
ECHO THAT IS MINE ALL MINE.

I curl myself up in the direction in which it feels like loneliness is breaking my body. I howl noiselessly, trying to expel the feeling without risking the dreaded knock of concern on my bedroom door. But the home that loneliness has carved out for itself within me is infinite, and it fills that home completely.

I can't remember when I stop feeling like this. I only realise that I have about a year later when a newly sober friend calls me and through the phone I can hear that same loneliness in the background, its silent yet sonorous heartbeat. I hear it again over other phone calls with other newly sober people, and each time I feel powerless because all I can weakly say is, 'it'll pass.' 'It's shit, but it'll pass.'

I wonder now whether it's less that loneliness passes and more that we pass through it.

Marjorie Suchocki, a process theologian, writes of loneliness as a passageway between two different forms of relation. The first consists of the day-to-day relationships we have with each other. Be the 'other' human or non-human, animate or inanimate, the exchanges we have are both inexorable and essential to our ability to make meaning out of the world. Yet sometimes, these relationships lose their texture. For whatever reason, they become levelled to a meaningless sameness, and in these moments we feel as though we're on the outside looking in. We feel lonely.

In this state, loneliness can alert us to a second kind of relation. The 'inaccessible depth' of kinship we can have with God, which we sense but have yet to grasp.[1] Ordinarily, when surface-level relationships are textured and meaningful, this sense of God is hard to discern. Its omnipresence paradoxically renders it hidden from our awareness because we don't have its absence to compare it to. But when finite experiences lose their texture, become devalued and un-diverse, suddenly a new contrast emerges, '[touching] the edges of consciousness'.[2]

As it surfaces, loneliness appears as a reflection of our desire for deeper relation. It's a way of intuiting the potential of something more with a God who is usually hidden in 'the dailiness of life'.[3] Following this desire—understanding loneliness as this passageway between earthly relation and divine relation—can lead us directly to God and the kind of relationship that triumphs over loneliness.

Miraculously, this is not the end in itself. God is a materialist. That is, God is fundamentally concerned with offering 'redemptive possibilities to the world'.[4] Thus, the point is not to make an inward journey solely in order to commune with God in solitude. Rather, to move towards God's presence is to immediately be flung back into 'the relationality of the everyday world'.⁵ To conform to God's divine purpose is neces-sarily to continue engaging in the meaning-making process that's entailed in day-to-day relationships. This is what we're freed from loneliness to do.

So, what of addiction? And specifically of early recovery—that point along the crip timeline of knowing loneliness more visceral than anything I'd felt before or have felt since.

Alfred North Whitehead, progenitor of process philosophy, and theologians who are influenced by his work define process as an open metaphysics—a theory of reality that must continu-ally be tested against all elements of reality and adapted wher-ever contradictions arise. Suchocki used process to produce the generic description of loneliness as passageway; upon finding that it spoke to my recovery experience, I wanted to test it a little against the reality of addiction. Not only did it hold up, but it also addressed loneliness's part in a wider reality of coming to political consciousness.

The chase

The first few months of sobriety were characterised by the total flattening of finite relation, its utter devaluation. They followed a lifetime of trying to make the finite infinite. Not just with alcohol, but with everything.

It's low tea, held in my secondary school's sparse dining hall. I've come alone but manage to bump into not only Phil, but Grace and Jeremy as well. I feel a rush of excitement and gratitude, the thrill of unexpectedly encountering people you love. We sit and talk for the full half hour until a member of staff says it's time to go. The devastation must be clear on my face because Jeremy says something along the lines of 'this was never going to last forever'. I get a sense of déjà vu, albeit one calling from the future rather than the past. 'But it should,' I think.

Pre-recovery, the infinite always connoted oblivion. Tumbling endlessly into the contentment of the first bite of something good or into that initial burst of light when you round a corner and catch sight of your best friend. To do that requires no longer being of the rest of the world. Existing in that moment forever requires you to go it alone, because taking anyone or anything else in there with you invites the possibility of change, of an ending. Part of me must always have understood that relation begets meaning because that desire to exist outside of relation in order to enjoy the infinite felt like a desire for the destruction of all time, matter and signification. Like a desire for oblivion.

But neither time nor matter has ever done what I've wanted. The first bite always dissolves. Each ensuing moment with that friend is wonderful but also takes you further away from that burst of light.

So begins the chase. Because in the same instant that you understand that the first can't last, you believe that if you can just get the conditions exactly right, you can win over time and matter. You can make the finite infinite.

You start to spend time with your friends not so much for their company but because you're chasing that one dinner party that Christine threw that you can't stop thinking about. Where you learned that figs and honey are made for each other and everyone meshed together brilliantly and you felt essential to that enmeshment rather than ancillary or coincidental to it. And every dinner party she hosts after that is amazing but *just* fails to reach that height of intimacy, so you settle for a solitary recreation in a corner of the room with two bottles of wine and that familiar warmth creeping across your skull.

Maybe the conditions will be right on your fourth Deliveroo of the day and the Five Guys you order will be just like that afternoon with Susie back in 2014, the very first time you bit into a $5 burger that wasn't a $5 burger, contemplating a massive *GQ* review painted on the wall while the humid blue skies of Washington, DC, waited outside with the promise of nothing to do that day—that summer—but please yourself.

Or you grab your exhausted vibrator once again with the unconscious expectation that you'll be met with the kind of pleasure that only comes with the innocent wonder of masturbating those first few times as a pre-teen.

And, of course, there was the first drink, when you realised that you were finally home. Before then you had spent your life wandering the desert, and that drink made you feel human in ways you had never felt human before.

But unlike with the other firsts, with each drink that comes after, you realise that alcohol has its own magical ability to recreate that feeling of firsts across a range of experiences. Not quite a perfect reconstruction, but close enough. Over time, even this becomes less effective, and you run your life into the ground trying to bring that feeling back.

The chase ended once I got sober. The first few weeks passed uneventfully. Life quickly started to come together again. Then the loneliness began to build. First, this feeling of waiting for someone. A gap in my life that felt so tangible I assumed its shape was that of a person who had previously been there and was gone but would return any day now. I waited. Those who were coming back came back and I learned to carry on without those who weren't, but still the expectancy of a missing person somewhere out there persisted. I was dancing at a Black Pride afterparty when I realised that this someone was never coming because the absence wasn't the absence of a real person or thing. It was just an absence. A yawning rift between a then unrecognised call from God and a sudden awareness of the flatness of my day-to-day relationships.

It took much longer to recognise that these relationships had been flattened by the chase. Suchocki writes about how ordinarily our surface relationships—those interactions that are constitutive of the self—have varying values that fluctuate depending on what is of immediate importance to us.

She uses the example of a writer and her son. The son might be very important to his mother, but whenever she wrote, his importance to her might fade to the back of her mind as her work became of most value to her in that moment. This would reverse again when she stopped writing to have a conversation with him. 'Thus,' says Suchocki, 'daily existence admits a multitude of relationships, each with its own value, contrasted with the fluctuating purposes of existence.'[6]

During the chase, there was only one thing that mattered. Slowly but surely, all relationships and experiences lost their inherent value, and the only measure of their worth became their capacity to bring about the infinite. This was the sole, unfluctuating purpose of existence. I lived in search of the impossible. Unwilling to let life surprise me, I trekked well-travelled roads that led to guaranteed pleasure and ignored new avenues because they risked disappointment. Over time, all surface relation began to flatten until it became completely devalued. The universe shrank to the size of my bedroom as I sought to control all the conditions of my intoxication. I couldn't commit to anything or anyone except to the extent they might engender oblivion.

I think I'd have noticed the effects of this flattening sooner, that is, a feeling of loneliness might have stopped me, if it weren't for the numbing effect of alcohol. I sensed this growing loneliness vaguely while drunk, and when sobriety would bring about the feeling more acutely, I'd simply drink again.

And the chase created a texture of its own, waking me up every morning with the hope that this might be the day I learned how to make the first last. It got me out of bed. It's not that I was ignorant about the futility of the chase. Somewhere I always knew. But alcohol's effectiveness at bringing me close but not quite to the feeling of firsts meant denial had a comfortable living space, room enough to stretch its legs.

Once alcohol was gone, the futility of my life-long project laid itself bare. Denial fled, and all the relationships built on the chase revealed themselves to be flat. I had deprived myself for years of the ability to derive meaning from the world as it actually was, rather than as I needed it to be. Active addiction was an intermediary, a translator between myself and the world that relayed the world back to me as either a promise or a denial of the infinite. Without it, I found myself a stranger in a strange land, able to understand the language of relation spoken around me but not to speak it myself. I was alone in the worst way.

But while my understanding of the infinite wasn't real, its call very much was. I suspect that what I reduced to infinity was always simply God—I just wasn't recognising God as such.

In process theology, God's omnipresence isn't passive. God isn't quietly waiting for us to notice God in moments of loneliness. God is, instead, an inherent part of the relational process, present (albeit often at the level of the unconscious) for every moment of connection as a redemptive influence amongst many other influences. Our autonomy lies in our freedom to choose or not choose to respond to God's influence.

Maybe this is what I glimpsed in the encounters I wanted to make last forever. God present in the love of my friends, in the joys of junk food and orgasm, even in the Lethean pleasure of alcohol, all of which could conceivably have constituted positive responses to God's redemptive aim for myself and others in those first instances. But, assuming that's the case, I mistakenly attributed God's eternal quality to the very finite objects and interactions behind which God was shrouded. I mined them doggedly, damaging myself and others in the process, probably the only outcome that can come of devoting yourself to making things that are inherently bound and determinate endless.

Sobriety ended this mining process, forced me to sit in emotions I'd have preferred to escape. And so, a passageway emerged between these two phenomena: the ever-present call of God and the relationships flattened during my search for God in finitude. Without alcohol to hold the two together, I

59

found myself lying in bed for most of 2019, wondering if it was possible to die of loneliness.

With the help of a group of recovering alcoholics, I crossed that passageway. In meeting God, I was flung back into the world. At first this was within my recovery community, taking on responsibilities to reach out to others, sharing the little I'd learned so far with people more newly in recovery. Increasingly, it was also within the world at large.

The politics of loneliness

Back in the world, I see there are many other sources of loneliness beyond the chase. While I've tested Suchocki's analysis against an embodied and spiritual experience, many of loneliness's causes are in fact political.

Part of my being flung back into the world has involved volunteering at pro bono law centres and at a mental health hotline. Often, it's apparent early on in a call that there's little these services can do to help the caller, but they stay on the line simply to talk. To voice their frustrations, tell me about their day or their past lives. I hear a familiar, tangible loneliness through the phone, except this time it's caused by unsafe housing or poor medical treatment. I hear how isolating it feels to write to the housing authority, local MP, mayor of London, to be signposted from Shelter to the Law Society, to describe one's trauma for the umpteenth time to an expressionless bureaucrat, to find oneself in a police cell during an acute mental health crisis, all the while never once truly heard, let alone helped. To have the meaning-making process of day-to-day relation tell you loud and clear that your unliveable circumstances do not matter.

Loneliness is compounded by the fact that alienation abounds under capitalism, alienation not just from our labour but also from who we could be to each other. From time to time, I break up a long day at work with a call to my sister, or

I sit and gossip with my housemates late into the night. I feel the pains of the day leave me, but then I remember that in this moment too, I am being reproduced as a worker. I cannot extricate myself from the reality that every choice I make to engage in fulfilling relation also keeps me healthy enough to work for as long as I'm needed the next day. I'm free to decide which relationships build me back up again, to reject the primacy of the nuclear family and its demand to physically reproduce yet more workers, to be restored instead by friends and family of my choosing and on my own terms. There is freedom in this, but not enough to escape the gravitational pull of the eight-hour workday that dominates life.

A stream of articles have been written over the years on loneliness as an epidemic. That loneliness is a public health and social justice issue is not a new idea. I'm not convinced that our finite relationships with each other were ever meant to be so painful on such a large scale. An unexpected joy of loneliness can be the discovery of God, but I reject any idea that the pain of capitalist alienation is specifically willed by God to bring us closer to God. In being flung back to help enact God's will, I have, instead, the strong sense that it is to contribute whatever I can to make our finitude less painful. Not to eradicate loneliness (which is a normal and healthy emotion) but to chip away at its unacceptable causes, like racism, ableism, poverty, homophobia and transphobia, borders, ageism.

I think part of the key to this is engaging with loneliness as a passageway, this time one between the individual experience of oppression and the deeper knowledge that another world is possible. Capital is the social relation that flattens all other forms of relation that do not feed it. It strives to make itself the sole value against which all relationships are judged and devalues those relationships in the process. Yet in doing so, it alerts us to the possibility of something more. If loneliness is the mediation between surface and depth—a depth that is omnipresent but hard to discern—perhaps the desolation that characterises late capitalism is also the product of our under-standing, somewhere deep down, that this is not all that there is. Maybe something of the communist horizon (its affect or promise, its present experiments) already exists and is endlessly calling to us, obscured by the texture of relationships under capitalism that are comfortable and satisfying but fundamen-tally always characterised by lack.

The production of loneliness therefore appears to be another contradiction of capitalism. Loneliness is a shared language, one that can ultimately speak to the possibility of solidarity. We are all brought to our knees by the hand of the free market for different reasons, but the loneliness this engen-ders is communal. I have found friends and comrades as a direct result of shared loneliness caused by systems like racism and sexism. Together, we crossed the passageway of loneliness and were vindicated in our discovery that another world is indeed possible.

In loneliness, others have even begun to build that world. The irresistible consequence of encountering liberatory theory, the archive and world-builders who have travelled the passageway before us is that, thrown back into the world, we make a practical commitment to joining the effort.

Because it is, in fact, possible to die of loneliness. People are killed by loneliness and its causes every day. So, to the best of my ability, I try to heed the deep call of God and the new world (which to me are one and the same but need not be so to everyone), to feel the exhilarating rush of being flung back into finite relation, and to hit the ground running.

ALCOHOLICS AND
THE IMAGO DEI

I struggle to talk about addiction with Christians. To find a language to express how a relationship with God got and keeps me sober without feeding into a redemption narrative that conceives of active addiction as a time of sin.

I want to be able to talk about how active addiction felt like being at a distance from God without the risk of that being framed as a moral failing, a position 'good' Christians could never find themselves in.

My addiction is not a warning to the able of what might happen to them should they stray too far from God. Not an example to affirm the strength of their own faith; not a means of saying that ableness is close to Godliness and so a person's fall from grace can be measured by the extent of their disability or lack thereof. Addicts are not objects to be held up in front of congregations as evidence of how sick society has become to produce such abject things.

And I don't want my healing to be used to reinscribe ableist norms either. The purpose of my recovery is not to prove God's power to the non-disabled.

But I don't just reject the narrative of the addict's redemption arc because it's ableist. It's also because it fails to recognise how disability can itself be redemptive. It was a mutual aid society of alcoholics who got me sober, who used the knowledge they had gained of their own bodyminds—their own addict epistemologies—to get me well. And it's through my own experience of disability that I've best come to hear God and understand and enact God's will, for the most part, by helping other alcoholics get sober.

I'm not grateful to be disabled, but given that I am disabled, I'm grateful that it's been the means through which I've become able to immerse myself in the world in ways that weren't possible before. Many people are capable of being in the world, feeling their political commitments on a more-than-intellectual plane, communing with human and non-human others from a place of genuine vulnerability, without the need for abstinence from drugs. I struggled with those things before, and the journey from being unable to meet God as I was in active addiction to being better reconciled with God now has brought me closer to being in the world.

In any case, the redemption arc from disabled to non-disabled doesn't apply here. In recovery, I am still managing a disability. There are many people whose using might spiral in response to certain circumstances who are able to return to healthy drug consumption when these issues are resolved. There are others who choose not to use again but don't need to practise a recovery programme to maintain abstinence. I'm not one of them, which means that even with years of sobriety, the only way for me to maintain health is to abstain and participate in a recovery programme. Were I to stop treating my addiction, I would again become disabled in a way that would perhaps be more recognisable as disabled to others.

Then there's the social precarity that afflicts even recovered addicts, be it stigma, difficulties accessing healthcare, the risk of being fired or discriminated against due to the lack of adequate protection under employment law, or the criminalisation of drugs that renders relapses more dangerous than they need to be.

The fact that I've come through a transformative experience with God and emerged not only still disabled but understanding and enacting God's will through that disability tells me two things.

The first is that my disability is not an impediment to a connection to God but in fact participates fully in the imago Dei, or, broadly speaking, the image of God.

This is a truth drawn not only from experience but also from an engagement with faith through the lens of a liberatory theology of disability. Looking to the symbol of the crucified and resurrected Christ as explored by theologian and sociologist Nancy Eiesland, we see in Luke 24:36–39 that Jesus settled his disciples' doubts about whether he had been raised from the dead by showing them his impaired hands and feet. That is, he uses his disabled body as evidence of his Godly nature—a direct contradiction to an ableist social-symbolic order found in both the church and the wider world in which disability is associated with brokenness and sin. That Jesus's wounds were not erased upon his conquest of death, that his impairment was directly connected with his relation to God, tells me that it's not God's intention that my often difficult disabled body be disposed of in favour of a 'perfect' disability-free one, either in this world or in any that might follow. I participate fully, alcoholism and all, in the imago Dei alongside every other person.

This isn't to reify disability. It isn't even to say that if I were given the opportunity to be rid of alcoholism I'd reject it (I'd take up the chance in a heartbeat). It's simply to say that neither experience nor liberatory Biblical interpretation tells me that disability is sin or brokenness. Disability simply is. The inescapability of this simple fact might underlie part of the stigma around it. As writer Joan Tollifson points out, 'Life is the way it is, not the way we wish it was, and disability is a constant embodiment of this basic truth'.[1]

I believe in a materialist God. One whose primary tool is the world as it exists, not as humans wish it existed. This means that God must work through disability not to eliminate it or to inspire the non-disabled but in the same ways that God works through everything else in creation. Sometimes to produce a radical shift, sometimes to enact a quiet change unknowable even to the changed being itself, always in accordance with God's will and not the demands of the political economy of the day.

The second thing I learn is that my disability is as much the product of social structures as it is an embodied experience. A personal encounter with God, powerful as it might be, does not eradicate the infrastructure that creates disability, both as a social construct and as a material phenomenon. What that experience does tell me is that God is as concerned with social transformation as with personal transformation.

When I think about scriptural interpretations that uphold the status quo, the first that spring to mind relate to miracle stories. Accounts of Jesus healing sick and disabled people, like the paralysed man at Capernaum or the bleeding woman on the way to Jairus's house, have been used to convert new Christians and deepen the faith of existing ones. They have also been used to objectify disabled people and to blame their disabilities on a lack of faith.

Efforts to counter ableist readings of the miracle stories have focused on the point in the narratives when previously disabled people are restored to their communities. Their healing makes them able to participate in society without the restrictions of sickness and its alienating rules. It's been argued that we should engage with these stories more symbolically and understand that their most important aspect is that disabled people were brought back into the fold. Rather than fixating on curing disabled people, what we are actually being called to do is heal our communities by making them inclusive.

I value these interpretations, particularly when read in the light of arguments offered by postcolonial theologians like Sharon V. Betcher, who grapple with the Bible as a historical document and with the miracle stories as events that took place under empire. In *Spirit and the Politics of Disablement*, Betcher recognises that the Roman Empire, like all empires, was disabling. She writes that it was common for prisoners of war at that time to be physically disfigured as punishment and for that disablement to be used both as a marker of their social status and a means of preventing their escape. The nature of work for Rome's most marginalised citizens was disabling, and many of Jesus's followers will have been disabled.

In this political context, the liturgical refrain in the Gospels that 'the blind see, the lame walk, the deaf hear' is addressed directly to a disabled audience, although not to provide a simple promise of freedom from impairment. Rather, it can be read as a critique of and a threat to the Roman Empire and all colonising powers that produce disabled subjects. As Betcher writes, 'the fact that colonialism occasions disease and disability ... points precisely to the reason one must interrogate this notion of miracle as individual somatic remediation'.[2]

The liturgical refrain thus becomes a political mantra. Perhaps, as Betcher suggests, it is a means for dominated groups to communicate their hopes for revolution discreetly. Under a surveillance state, rebellious intent can be masked in this way beneath the seemingly innocuous desire for a reversion to health.

It makes me think of the Beatitudes taught by Jesus during his Sermon on the Plain in the Gospel of Luke. Promises include that the poor are blessed, for theirs is the kingdom of God, as are those who hunger, for they will be satisfied.[3] But Jesus also goes on to say:

But woe to you who are rich,
for you have received your consolation.
Woe to you who are full now,
for you will be hungry.
Woe to you who are laughing now,
for you will mourn and weep.[4]

God's promise is clear. It's not simply that our communities are to be healed by giving disabled people a seat at the table. If we understand healing in this context to be a form of justice, then we see that God's promise also envisages that empire and all its disabling elements will be turned upside down. Those who are first will be last, and the last first. As someone who is in many ways rich, full and laughing, it requires me to become invested in the losses that await me should I live to see a new world, to 'will [my] own destruction' as a necessary condition of the social transformation God aims to bring about, even as there are other ways I would only begin to be fully human in this new world.[5]

Turning the world upside down also requires us to understand that ability is as much a social construct as disability is. Late capitalism is invested in a particular vision of wholeness, and Christian theology has long been complicit in legitimising that vision.

Returning to Betcher, she reminds us that all too often, Christianity and its Holy Spirit are used to discipline people into the 'strictures of cultural ideology'.[6] The images of wholeness that are presented to us under capitalism become incorporated into Christian theology, repackaged as the will of God, and sold to us again in the language of spiritual fulfilment and faithfulness.

She goes on to write of wholeness as an eschatological illusion, that is, one relating to death and the afterlife. In a similar way, French psychoanalyst Jacques Lacan wrote of wholeness as a hallucination associated with the mirror stage. The way I understand it, this reflection of the wholeness that will be ours in the afterlife becomes internalised in the living, an archetype towards which we strive and into which we attempt to discipline ourselves and others. But this wholeness isn't real. It's mediated by the demands of capital (be able enough to work, be an individual with no need for relation beyond that which reproduces you as a worker) and has little to do with a God who calls us to love and be loved by the stranger and to struggle for justice, not profit.

If this wholeness is an illusion, it must be one for everyone, disabled or non-disabled. A disabled lens might be what ends up exposing the myth, but this discovery has implications for us all. Recognising ability/wholeness as a social construct and not a God-given gift or instruction would end the disciplining process we might be putting ourselves through. It would allow Christians to divest from late-capitalist and neo-colonial conditions and force us to ask more interesting questions about what God has determined is good for us and for the world. It would open a way for us to grapple with what it means not to be of the world but still be invested in it. To not participate in its brutality and to change it at the same time.

Least of all these consequences is that churches would finally feel like a safe environment for discussing addiction. If none of us are whole or broken and are instead all committed to healing a broken world, Christianity becomes a project that allows for expansive conversations about what healing looks like. Without the ableist narratives. Without the redemption arc.

A BLACK FEMINIST GOD

SATURDAY, 3 NOVEMBER 2018

I'M STRUGGLING WITH SOME OF THE WORK MY SPONSOR'S GIVEN ME SO AM READING AUDRE LORDE. I SENSE MY CONCEPTION OF GOD NEEDS TO CHANGE IN A FUNDAMENTAL WAY BUT I'M NOT YET SURE WHICH WAY. IT WAS ALREADY A REVELATION TO DISCOVER THAT GOD LOVES ME REGARDLESS OF WHETHER I DRINK AND HE WANTS ME TO GET BETTER EVEN WHEN I DON'T WANT TO GET BETTER. BUT EVEN WRITING THE NAME GOD EVOKES A DISTANCE I'M TRYING TO GET RID OF ...

AS MUCH AS I'M ENJOYING READING PAUL'S LETTERS IN THE NEW TESTAMENT, MAYBE PART OF THE ISSUE IS THAT I'M TRYING TO SWALLOW AN ENTIRE THEOLOGY WHEN AT THIS POINT THINGS NEED TO BE SIMPLER? IS GOD WHAT I NEED RIGHT NOW? WOULD HE BE ANGRY IF I TURNED TO BLACK FEMINISM PRIMARILY AT THIS POINT WHILE STILL PRAYING TO HIM? WHAT DOES IT MEAN TO NOT WANT HIS HELP FROM THE START? I FEEL TERRIBLE AND ANXIOUS ABOUT IT, BUT EVERYTHING IN ME SETTLES WHEN I THINK ABOUT FOCUSING ON USING BLACK FEMINISM TO PULL ME OUT OF THIS FOR NOW.

It settled over the memory of turning to Lola at the feminist book club meeting and introducing myself. Of stumbling over my fresher feet trying to keep up with Priscilla's brisk walk down Senate House Passage as she instructed me to begin first with *Zami*, then *Sister Outsider*, and had I read any bell hooks yet?

It settled over the embodied warmth of a FLY meeting, organised by the network for women and non-binary people of colour at my university. That magic that hangs in the air wherever catharsis and political consciousness–raising meet. Where you come to grips with the reality of oppression and in the same moment realise you're not alone. It was life-giving. I came the closest I had ever got to feeling like I belonged somewhere.

God, on the other hand, was a solitary matter. I had church, but by 2018 I was last in, first out on a Sunday morning. Vaguely aware that the God I had inherited was shrouded behind layers of punishing indoctrination, I picked away at them with split-ting nails in crouched isolation. I could read and be moved by what Paul had to say about love and grace, but I knew what really felt like it had me in its hand. What had brought me a found family worth living for, what I believed when it told me that on the other side of addiction was Life with a capital 'L'. And it wasn't the possessive, angry source of conditional love I'd been raised with.

So, I switched them out. God for black feminism.

The results were mixed.

I'm paused on my bike at the top of Tulse Hill, considering whether to turn right down my street or carry on twenty or so metres further to the Tesco Express. I was stopped by the police five minutes ago for allegedly running a red light, even as behind us traffic continued to flow past a light that was obvi-ously glowing green. Evidently, they were having a slow night. The stakes were low and, as I expected, they let me go after a few minutes of flexing their power, but I feel indignant. I want to drink. Then I think of Ruth Wilson Gilmore's definition of racism.[1] I consider the history of the state reaching its long arms into the homes of black alcoholics and killing them via the bottle. My bike makes the turn to the right, takes me home. I lay my head on the pillow that night sober and triumphant.

The next morning, I'm back on that corner waiting for the bus to uni, which is running over fifteen minutes late. I'm now guaranteed to miss the bulk of my first lecture, and there's only one more after that, which means the day's a bit of a write-off; no point going all the way in for just an hour. A bubbling excitement begins to grow in me and I pretend it isn't there. My feet start to walk me away from the bus stop and I urge them to go right when I get to my street.

'Home,' I hiss under my breath as they approach the turn.

'Home,' I whisper more quietly as they cross the road instead.

'Home,' I sigh in the aisle of cool bottles to the promise of an early end to the day.

I'm not the first person to try to use black feminism's power to pull me out of active addiction. There will be thousands of others, like the 'little sister from AA' who stood up during one of Audre Lorde's poetry readings one afternoon in 1986 and 'talked about how much courage [Lorde had] given her'. Lorde reflects in *A Burst of Light* that it made her think of 'all those intricate connections between us [black women] by which we sustain and empower each other'.[2] These connections *are* powerful; doubtless they are sufficient to save some, but not so for me.

What I went on to learn from my failed experiment, however, was that the relation between black feminism and God wasn't either-or, or one now and another later. It was always both.

Black feminism taught me about the love I deserved, showed me what grace looked like in practice. It occurred to me at some point that, unsatisfied as I was with the God I'd inherited, I did believe it was a God that brought me to black feminism. Turning to Lola at the book club, believing Priscilla when she said I'd make a good FLY facilitator, trusting my newly discovered ability to make gatherings of people into healing spaces, none of those instincts ever felt in the moment like they came from within me. In many ways, these decisions were unlike me, but I felt called to make them anyway.

Abandoning everything I thought I knew about God, I started from scratch, beginning solely with that single thread: only something that loved me could have drawn me towards a political ideology and community that had given me so much. In trying to discern God anew, I judged God against black feminist principles. The longer I did so, the clearer it became that God not only met but exceeded its standards. Black feminism became a light that God turned to Godself to show me what had always been there but had been obscured by punitive and patriarchal teachings: a God that was unconditionally loving and deeply concerned with social change.

Unlike the God in the diary entry above, now shockingly unrecognisable to me, this was a God I could let close to me in my pain. The only God capable of transforming my life in all the ways it's been transformed. God as the source of novelty in my life, pulling me out of old habits and into unexpected directions, graciously presenting me with redemptive influences that have the capacity to save my life—one of which was the call to black feminism.

SHAME

I was supposed to write about shame here.

About how to rebuild a life from the ashes of shame. How to come to, suddenly, in a life from which you have already decided not to run. What happens when the buzzing stops and you're left with a silence that marks the beginning of the rest of your life. How to say out loud without rescinding it that the love of your friends saved your life. What it is to hesitate around the corner from the pub where your friends have gathered and to know that you will have to stand there for hours amongst people who have seen you more naked than you have seen yourself and make casual conversation. What it's like to text back, and text back again, each text a commitment to stay, a concrete stone wedged into the mud of shame. How to limit yourself to two calls a day to your sponsor, asking how a mind holds this much shame without unravelling, and hear back every time, 'This, too, shall pass.'

But the essay wouldn't come.

I stood near the top of a hill and I called to it, to the open sky. I knelt by the couch, lowered my face to mere millimetres from the ground, peered into the dusty gloom and beckoned to it. I reached for it when one day it swam across my collarbones but it slipped through my fingers. I watched it bend, turn and swim down to my belly, out of sight again. I wrote it and deleted it. I teased it gently with my fingernails as if peeling paint from the wall and it broke apart in my hands. I sang to it, hoping that with the vibrations of my ribcage it would emerge scowling, eyes blinking in the light.

And it wouldn't come.

Instead, I have the memory of S's voice in my ear as I stand on the corner of the street before it turns on to the pub where my friends have gathered. She is telling me about her boyfriend trouble as we both wait for courage to find me. There is B giving me life-saving advice that he says I gave him months ago although I have no memory of it now. M telling me people change. And the rows and rows of houses that surround us. All built on concrete stones wedged one by one in the mud of shame. Solid, somehow, and shining.

LOVE IS A DOING WORD

There's this saying that the opposite of addiction is connection. When I dig into how that relates to what I know about addiction as an embodied thing, the conclusion I get to is that love and addiction can't sit next to each other; one always immobilises the other.

By which I mean that love is always two things: a state of being and an ethical responsibility. It's that desire for someone else's good, which may or may not also be tied to a desire to be around them, and the actions that we take to facilitate their flourishing.

It's the responsibility part that I found addiction constantly rendered inert. I could look at someone for whom I knew I had great feeling yet not be able to *do* anything with that feeling. Not call her when I knew she was lonely, not turn up when they asked me to, not treat him in the ways he deserved.

In the bubble of the it's-not-time, the usual rules of cause and effect were broken. Just as with pain and change, the two halves of love decoupled and it became effectively meaningless. Because even then I was uninterested in a definition of love that didn't include both the feeling and the doing. The internal logics that tied separate events to each other were replaced with a constant mediation of those events by addiction. That is, whether it made sense to connect A to B became less about B's relationship to A and more about whether connecting the two would facilitate the search for the infinite. If the answer was no, then A and B floated by each other indifferently. It meant that where love and addiction were concerned, addiction immobilised love, ensuring that as far as possible, it could be nothing more than a feeling.

If I were to reduce what my recovery entails to one phrase, it would be making sure that now it's always love that's immobilising addiction. Upon finally leaving the it's-not-time, I was brought into a temporal logic where love as an ethical responsibility could flourish again. Cause and effect returned, but a new thing came with it: an awareness that I'm not truly separate from anything or anyone, nor have I ever been. The pain I experienced and caused in active addiction was in part the product of my compulsive participation in a myth of separation that simply wasn't reflective of real life.

It took a lot of time to strengthen that ethical muscle; I'm still working on it. And none of this is to abdicate responsibility for being so unloving in the past. Love as a verb necessarily entails accountability. But the principles of recovery I follow, which centre relation so strongly, are primarily concerned with love as a doing word. As long as I live in sober time, love continues to immobilise addiction.

ABOLITION

Addiction produces a healthy assemblage of contradictory narratives in public discourse. This is perhaps most clearly seen in legal and public health policy on drug use in countries like the UK and the USA, where addicts are presented as sick people in need of well-funded health services yet also targeted by a punitive state. Abolitionists have long grappled with this contradiction, and given that carceral solutions to addiction are as violent as they are ineffectual, addicts are often invoked as a reason that prisons should be abolished. These invocations are fruitful in that they invite us to imagine radically different social frameworks for helping some of the most marginalised members of society, and they are often made by people who have themselves been criminalised for drug use or addiction. While I'm also interested in looking further, asking what an addict epistemology might contribute to how we imagine a world without prisons, let's start by considering some of the abolitionist arguments against the criminalisation of drug use.

The war on drug users

In the UK, addiction is inherently criminalised by virtue of anti-drugs legislation like the Misuse of Drugs Act 1971 (MDA). The MDA creates a category of 'controlled drug', of which possession or sale (among other activities) is criminalised. Substances in this category include stimulants, hallucinogens and depressants; these are then sub-categorised into different classes with graded levels of severity in their associated penalties.

Without the ability to purchase drugs legally, a person who is actively addicted to any of these controlled substances risks being pulled into the state's carceral apparatus as punishment for a compulsion outside of their control. They are automatically drawn into an underground economy that presents dangers to their safety even aside from the threat of criminalisation: under these conditions, the quality and safety of drugs cannot be regulated, putting all drug users at risk. Criminalisation also means people with problematic illicit drug use are less willing to seek help. Only one in twenty young people interviewed as part of a 2016 survey by the Royal Society of Public Health 'felt confident that they would receive the help they would need for illegal drug use without judgment'.[1] When accessing public healthcare is entangled with the risk of being branded a criminal, addicts who need help are effectively abandoned by the state.

Criminalisation also leads to disproportionate police harassment and punishment of communities of colour, especially black people.[2] Depending on a number of factors (including class, race and whether your magistrate had a good breakfast that morning), a person can be punished for their drug use with criminal sanctions ranging from a discharge to several years' imprisonment, all of which carry a criminal record. Black people are arrested at a higher rate than white people following stop and search and given out-of-court disposals at a lower rate, despite the detection rate from stop and search being similar across ethnic groups. Major discrepancies arise as specifically concerns cannabis possession, with black and Asian people being convicted at 11.8 and 2.4 times the rate of white people respectively in 2017, in spite of lower rates of self-reported cannabis use.[3] Discrimination abounds even before drug possession has been established; the rate that black people are stopped and searched by police is six times that of their white counterparts, increasing to nine times when the reason given is suspected drug possession.[4]

Beyond its racist application, it's also clear from the history of the law that anti-drugs legislation and policy are inherently racialised.[5] Controls on the possession and unlicensed import or export of cocaine, opium and heroin were first introduced in the UK under the 1920 Dangerous Drugs Act as a wave of Sinophobic hysteria was rolling through London. The high-profile overdose in 1918 of Billie Carleton, a young and celebrated English theatre performer, sparked a racist drugs scandal as her death was linked to a Chinese resident of Limehouse, a slum by the Thames that was home to London's first Chinatown.[6] This hysteria had its corollaries in the USA, where an obsession with Chinese migrants led to the country's earliest recorded drug law (the 1875 San Francisco opium den ordinance), as well as in western Canada at the turn of the twentieth century, where moral panics over the drug use of Chinese migrants also emerged.[7] The UK's own moral panic persisted throughout the 1920s as London's Chinese population was increasingly associated with drugs and criminality and presented as a threat to white womanhood.[8] The consequent desire to police this community took legal shape in the form of drugs legislation that emerged around this time.

Racist hysteria over drugs intensified again in the 1950s and 1960s, as London's jazz scene began to be associated with drug use, and journalists expressed fears around social mixing between black and white youth. Again, racialised men, this time black, were presented as pushing drugs onto innocent white women.[9] The emergence of 'hippie' culture in the Sixties and its association with cannabis and LSD fuelled this panic and contextualises the ratification of a new Dangerous Drugs Act in 1964, which banned the cultivation of cannabis.[10]

There is significantly more history to uncover and more to be said on the death-making venture that is the UK government's latest foray into the 'war on drugs'. The point I'm briefly introducing is that while the state would have us believe that anti-drugs legislation is a just and proportionate response to the criminal behaviour of drug users, this is simply not true. It has always been a weapon used to police communities of colour, particularly where fears of mixing between white and non-white populations exist. To those who might argue that legislation like the MDA exists to protect drug users from themselves, this has also been shown to be patently false, as 2021 heralded the ninth year in a row in which the number of drug-related deaths rose in the UK.[11]

The problems with reform

Attempts have been made to reform the criminal justice system under the logic that addicts should be met with a softer response from the law. The first problem with this line of reasoning is that it entrusts the care of people struggling with chaotic substance use to the same system that has been set up to criminalise addiction in the first place and that is flagrantly racist, classist and misogynistic. Nor can we assume the criminal justice system to be capable of addressing issues around housing and employment, which play central roles in recovery, when its reaction to people's responses to homelessness or poverty is often to criminalise those, too.

The second problem with the logic of reform to help addicts is that it requires a distinction between non-problematic, recreational drug users, who deserve harsh sentences, and addicts, who deserve care. But no one should be criminalised for drug use, including people who can use safely, who happen to account for the overwhelming majority of drug users. The importance of rejecting such a distinction becomes especially clear when we consider that the law is both reflective and constitutive of social norms that make us intelligible to the state and to each other. Distinctions made under the law have a way of haunting us even outside their legal contexts.

Moreover, to suggest that there are only two categories of drug user—the totally unproblematic and the problematic—robs people of the ability to evaluate their relationship to drugs, which inevitably changes over the course of one's life, with self-love and curiosity as opposed to anxiety. The benefits and harms that can come from drug use, and whether and how they arise, are highly contingent on our environments and moods, and as these change and shift, so too can our relationships to drugs and the effects they have on our lives. This is true of any drug we might consume, be it caffeine or LSD. Free of the addict/non-addict binary, we could more easily consider and negotiate our personal relationship to drugs as we do other day-to-day markers of health like diet or hygiene. A public health response to drug use could take a similar approach.

The addict/non-addict distinction also pathologises addiction in a way that is often not useful for addicts under the current status quo. The recognition of my addiction as an illness within the medical industry has put me at risk of involuntary sectioning, left me the recipient of open contempt from medical professionals, and led to the dismissal of the knowledge I have about my own bodymind in favour of the epistemically dominant opinions of psychiatrists.

In any case, like many liberal reforms of the criminal justice system, reformist attempts to help addicts have in practice only served to draw more people into the prison-industrial complex. Given that prisons are notoriously poor at facilitating recovery, reformers have made pushes to keep addicts out of detention, but their alternatives have in fact tended to expand the powers of the state's carceral apparatus and have ultimately proven harmful to all drug users and addicts.

An example of one such failed experiment is the Dublin Drug Treatment Court (DDTC), set up in 2001 to redirect non-violent offenders of drug-related crimes from prisons. At the time, 'tough-on-crime' rhetoric was becoming increasingly popular in Ireland, and drug courts were presented as a liberal approach to dealing with drug users, appealing to populist desires for punishment but also aligned with a general trend towards harm reduction across Europe.[12] The goal was for offenders who arrived in these courts to be directed to court-sanctioned treatment for drug use rather than made to face the inflexible criminal sanctions that are handed down in mainstream courts.

In fact, clear issues have been raised around the DDTC's expansion of the remit of the criminal justice system. Judges themselves have expressed concerns over the excessive power that they are given in the DDTC to set aside due process. In one case, sociology professor James Nolan reported that a new DDTC judge felt uncomfortable with recommendations to sanction a client for shoplifting according to the court's point system, which could lead to a custodial sentence, 'without giving the defendant a chance to challenge the charge in a more formal adjudicative process', under which the judge believed that the client 'probably would have gotten off'.[13]

Although claims have been made since as early as 2010 that the DDTC has largely failed to achieve its goals, civil servants have stated that it persists because it is 'politically popular', allowing politicians to appear simultaneously tough on drug-related crime and compassionate to addicts.[14] Cloaked behind a thin veil of 'harm reduction', the war on drugs progresses towards what has always been its aim: drawing marginalised communities (including addicts) deeper into the criminal justice system.

One clear illustration of the contradiction between the state's rhetoric of harm reduction and the reality of drug policy is the centrality of abstinence in its rehabilitative programmes. In brief, harm reduction is an approach that aims to reduce the harms associated with drugs for people who are 'unable or unwilling to stop' using them, for example through safe needle exchanges. It is based on a recognition of the funda-mental fact that 'many people throughout the world continue to use psychoactive drugs despite even the strongest efforts' to prevent this.[15] Consequently, any drug policy that denies this reality and centres abstinence as the desired end-goal of recovery cannot meaningfully claim to be harm-reductionist.

Rather than pressuring people to stop, a true harm-reductionist approach would be one that called for greater flexibility in the treatment of addiction and engagement with drug use in general at a public health level. It would seek to abolish the addict/non-addict binary and address drug use in all its complexity. This means beginning from the understanding that drugs can and do improve people's lives—that's why people take them. If I'd experienced the same effects from my very first drink that I was getting by my last, I would simply have stopped and never gone on to develop a compulsive relationship with the substance. For the first year or so, I drank alcohol because it made me feel good, made it easier to talk to people—all the same reasons why most people drink and consume other drugs. To start with the view of drug use as inherently problematic and then build a public health framework from there is a political choice, and one that simply isn't rooted in reality.

A harm-reductionist approach might openly acknowledge drug pleasure as the point of drug use. Harm-reduction advocate Chloe Sage makes a comparison with discourse around safe sex; although historically taboo, discussing sexual pleasure while disseminating information on how to prevent pregnancy or the spread of STIs is now part of the mainstream conversation.[16] Sage argues that a similar shift is needed in drug safety discourse, and I agree. The first thing I tell anyone who confides in me that they're worried about their drinking is that drugs are supposed to be fun. If you're not having fun anymore, that's reason enough to re-assess your relationship to them. Not from an anxious, self-critical place, but from a curious and self-compassionate one.

In terms of recovery, I see much of it now as pertaining to pleasure maximisation. I am happier when I don't drink and when I practise the principles of recovery across all areas of my life. Of course, when I first got sober, recovery was entirely about reducing harm and misery because my drinking had taken me to a place where harm and misery defined my life. But today, recovery is about maximising serenity and pleasure.

If we understand that people start using drugs because they offer something beneficial, abstinence stops making sense as the only solution for the subset of drug users who then find themselves unable or unwilling to stop even in the face of overwhelming harm. We can reduce the harm associated with occupying the it's-not-time and then, once we are safe, begin to consider what a healthy and pleasurable life for addicts might look like and try to go about building it. We can grapple with the desires underpinning each person's drug use, explore the material conditions that have shaped those desires or prevented them from being realised, and go from there.

ACCOUNTABILITY

As well as considering addicts as people in need of care, I'm also interested in addressing addicts as subjects in conversations about abolition. For people like me who spent active addiction behaving harmfully, much of the work of recovery could offer practical suggestions for experiments in transformative justice. What can addict knowledges contribute to the creative process of developing communities without a need for prisons?

Far from simply arguing for the destruction of punishing institutions, transformative justice reconfigures what counts as harm, focuses on the healing of those who have been harmed, addresses the underlying causes of harm in order to reduce its reoccurrence, and holds those who cause harm accountable whilst still upholding their humanity and dignity. In discussing transformative justice, I draw from Liat Ben-Moshe's analysis of disability as an optic that 'deconstructs the normative body/mind and uncovers the radical potential of living otherwise'.[1] I want to treat addict epistemology as a counterhegemonic force, one that destabilises the notion that the neurotypical mind is the best tool for imagining a better future and that draws on the ways that addicts already live otherwise to make suggestions for how everyone could live otherwise in communities governed by transformative justice.

I say 'ideas' because what transformative justice can and will look like in practice is complex and cannot fully be known. Every abolitionist experiment I've encountered has prompted entirely new questions. Each outcome has been laced with unpredictability. If I bring up a visual image of transformative justice, it is an unstable ball of violently vibrating energy. It is young—millennia old but still neonatal—and flashes of light streak erratically across its surface. Yet it holds together because this is precisely how it is meant to be. I maintain a nebulous relationship with Marxist teleology, but certainly at this stage of capitalism, the conditions for transformative justice to steady itself and flourish in this part of the world have yet to come. And even when they arrive, current experience suggests that transformative justice approaches will be highly situationally dependent. Today's standardised approach to justice will become unintelligible.

So, even as I identify and draw from an addict epistemology, I commit to Ben-Moshe's idea of abolition as dis-epistemology. That is, as a practice of letting go of the desire for certainty. This ostensible tension between knowing and not knowing is resolvable because so much of the addict experience is rooted in not knowing. Picking up the first drink not knowing if I'll surface from blackout in my bedroom or somewhere on the other side of London and drinking anyway. Outliving myself in recovery; waking up every morning having got to the very edge of the universe as I imagined it in active addiction and now living in the unknowable darkness of whatever it is the universe is expanding into.

From this perspective, it is easier to set light to the belief that we can't let go of carceral politics until we have a blueprint for what comes next and a guarantee that it will work. Abolition is about experimentation, and failure will inevitably play its part. The suggestions below could play a role in these experiments, alongside the countless other undertakings in transformative justice that blossom and disappear across the globe. I see those experiments as seeds that store the future within them. They should be cultivated.

I come to this conversation specifically as an addict who caused a lot of harm in active addiction and who, through their recovery programme, is engaged in a continuous act of transformation. By this I don't mean transformation into a different, better person. I see identity less in terms of linear narrative, more as palimpsest. All versions of me, including those that caused consistent harm, exist contemporaneously and could re-emerge as dominant should I and/or my conditions allow. With this in mind, I see transformation as a daily commitment to tend to all parts of myself. To nourish what is itself nourishing and to listen to those parts of myself that would otherwise make themselves known in antisocial ways, all the while understanding that I do this work to care for myself and to ensure I contribute positively to my communities in equal measure. This transformation is only possible when all parts of myself are brought to light to the greatest extent possible, and accountability is one such source of light. This also requires me to grapple with what social norms and structures facilitated the harm I caused and to become actively invested in their destruction.

In writing about this, I want to stress that I have no interest in deepening stigma against addicts. The majority of those whom I have encountered are themselves victims of harm, trauma and abuse. In this instance, I'm choosing to theorise truthfully from my experience because I think it offers practically useful insights for transformative justice. I think it's important to wring the use out of everything, even the things that are uncomfortable, precisely because of the urgency entailed by the fact that stigma kills. If the stigma surrounding addicts justifies their incarceration, which in turn reinforces the prison-industrial complex, then it makes sense to try to recapture uncomfortable stories of addiction and prevent them from being used in service of state violence. This takes the inevitability out of things. It keeps the powers that be from unilaterally determining what lessons can be learned from harm; it keeps them from having a monopoly over meaning. It is work that absolutely must take place alongside policy work to diminish this stigma, and each should cede to the other where appropriate and most useful.

Recovery has taught me that abolitionist work is affective work. This isn't to say that it's about emotional satisfaction. In fact, organiser and educator Mariame Kaba explicitly writes that 'abolition is not about your feelings'.[2] She gives the example of the imprisonment of singer R. Kelly on multiple counts of sexual abuse, explaining that abolition is not about feeding our drive to feel pleasure from seeing someone who has caused harm punished, but rather that it's about 'transforming the conditions in which we live, work, and play such that harm at the scale and as prolonged as that perpetrated by R. Kelly cannot develop and cannot be sustained.'[3] Abolition isn't about gratifying our emotional desires, but I don't think understanding this is at odds with knowing that feelings must also be grappled with in any transformative justice project. Here, rather than contending with the emotions of those seeking justice, I want to confront the emotions of those who perpetrate harm.

I'll start with shame. Not to argue, as is often done, that the shame or remorse of those who cause harm should be weighed against the emotional and material consequences for those who have been harmed. Nor to identify shame as a starting point from which all accountability journeys must begin. I start with shame simply because shame *is*. As we transform society from one that relies on punitive solutions to harm to one that seeks to address it productively, our affective responses to being held accountable will undoubtedly shift for the better. But shame is a human, enlightening response to causing harm, and it will continue to persist at the communist horizon. Transformative justice processes should account for this and not operate on the assumption that a 'good' comrade would never be plagued with emotions that render accountability difficult.

The process of accountability that I entered in recovery was led by someone who had herself caused harm and subsequently committed to the same process that I was now undergoing. As we discussed the harm that I'd caused, my sponsor confided that she too had done almost everything that I had done. This went a long way toward countering the shame I carried, which was preventing me from being honest with myself and others about the damage I had done.

Shame made me hope for punishment rather than accountability. Because punishment is something that takes a person outside of their community. It says, 'you have broken the rules that made you one of us, and now, different, alienating rules must be applied to you.' When someone feels at their most abject, being outside of community can be easier than being held. Accountability is the harder route where shame is concerned. It involves being seen, and it involves changing.

My sponsor understood this shame intimately. Her recognition that shame is a common response to committing harm, alongside her knowledge that this shame should not be made the concern of those who had been harmed, enabled her to tangibly give voice to bell hooks' assertion that we have to 'hold people accountable and yet at the same time remain in touch with their humanity enough to believe in their capacity to be transformed'.[4] Addressing shame strikes me as an essential element in any accountability process that recognises the humanity of its participants. It is part of the abolitionist promise to start work from the margins—to structure our abolitionist experiments first with those considered least capable or worthy of transformation in mind—because it is in these cases, especially where serious harm is concerned, that shame is more likely to arise as an issue. And yet we begin at the margins precisely because the marginal often finds a way of concerning everyone. I would be surprised if any reader could say they had never failed to apologise for causing minor harm out of shame or pride, its cousin. As long as we ensure that those who have been harmed are being centred in our transformative justice projects, we can also acknowledge the inevitability and humanity of shame for those who have harmed. My sponsor's help in addressing my shame played a direct role in my ability to become willing and able to be held accountable by the people I'd harmed.

What my experience also suggests is that there is a role for people who have caused harm in the practice of transformative justice. There's an extent to which this goes without saying. Everyone has caused harm, and so there can be no transformative justice process that doesn't involve people who have caused harm. But more specifically, a person's ability to draw from their experience of having caused harm can give them new knowledge that can enable someone else's transformation. Again, this practice should also include those people at the margins who have engaged in the work of transformative justice having caused serious harm.

This idea might make us uncomfortable when we're accustomed to a system under which the only forms of accountability for people who cause serious harm are punitive, even though carceral institutions ultimately do little to meaningfully prevent people from causing future harm. Recovery, however, creates spaces that promise more than what the state is capable of offering. Spaces where I have seen that transformation is genuinely possible. Where I trust that I can learn from people who have caused a lot of harm in the past, as others trust that they can learn from me. This is why I consider recovery to be an abolitionist experiment.

Shame is not the only affective response to recovery work that should be moulded into transformative justice projects. There is also hope. More important than the honesty my sponsor's experience fostered was the fact that she wasn't engaging in those behaviours anymore. She was evidence not only that I could push through shame but also that I could change. She laid out what her process of transformation looked like, and what she'd learned from others' transformations, as a road map that I could follow. Central to this was the assertion that transformation is not a one-time event. Whenever amends are made, work must be done before that point so that it can be a voluntary and honest experience. The work also has to be continued afterwards, through addressing the root causes of harmful behaviour so as to mitigate their impact on our lives and the lives of others as we move forward. What this transformation looks like will vary from person to person, but I've found the continuous nature of the work it involves to be freeing rather than disheartening. This is because it's simply less painful to continually work on myself than to constantly grapple with a dissonance between the person I want to be and the person I'm being.

Another element of addict knowledge that I draw from in this discussion responds to a question I frequently encounter: how do we trust a person who says they're transforming? I often hear people say that they believe in transformative justice but would never be able to trust anyone who had caused serious harm regardless of whatever accountability process they might have been through. I understand this instinct, and I used to feel the same way. But the addict epistemology formed in my recovery community changed my mind in two important ways.

The first relates to the tendency of people to be more inclined to trust a system than an individual. We see this clearly in the relationship that many people have with the criminal justice system. They don't necessarily understand how it works, but they trust that its workings are just. As abolitionists, we know this isn't true, but I wonder whether there might be something useful that can be taken from that trust. Maybe we can develop a more expansive definition of 'system', not a courthouse on a hill but a set of principles consistently but flexibly applied and enmeshed in the life of a community. Maybe trust in that system will develop over time as more people are exposed to its successes, which will require us to keep trying and keep tweaking in the face of inevitable failures. In this way, transformative justice might not necessarily ask us only to trust individuals but rather to trust a system that we have all brought into being, one that is of the community and that we have seen transform people over time.

The second idea that changed my mind runs a little deeper and does in fact allow us to assess whether we can trust individuals who claim to be in the process of transformation. In my experience, engaging in transformation has made me better able to tell whether someone else is transforming or simply adopting the language of transformation convincingly. Through undergoing the process myself, I not only know what tools a person who is transforming is supposed to be using. I also know how it *feels* to be transforming. When it hurts, when it frees. These affective responses leave a mark on the way I talk about transformation and the way that other addicts in recovery talk about it, too, which isn't present in the language of people who have yet to begin this process. And my own failures to act with integrity—my slip-ups—also teach me something about how and whom to trust.

In communities that centre transformative justice, we will all be transforming, and I think that will make us better able to make safe decisions about whom to trust. What I also think this presupposes is that the same basic accountability process must be used for all kinds of harm. While there will inevitably be some variations, there should not be an entirely separate process where 'serious' harm is concerned. This helps address the issue of shame, but it also helps build a community that can recognise transformation in others, because all of us will have been through the same process at various points in our lives and will have knowledge of what it is to transform.

Of course, there are no guarantees. By virtue of existing in relation with others we risk encountering people who seek to hurt us, and under no political economy can this risk be eradicated. But I don't believe the existence of this risk is reason enough to abandon the transformative justice project. After all, the alternative—criminal punishment—has not made us any less vulnerable to this risk. In fact, it exacerbates it.

*

My recovery community only offers a few pieces to add to the puzzle of how to create communities that render policing and prisons unnecessary. Given that this isn't its primary purpose, it's an imperfect source of knowledge on transformative justice. In some ways, the aims of the two projects are entirely at odds; my recovery programme explicitly rejects efforts to transform society (as opposed to individuals), while the primary focus of transformative justice is on structural change.

Another issue in my recovery community is that it is exclusive. I had mountains of support when making amends to people, but where those people have not been part of my recovery community, I've simply had to hope that they in turn had the support they needed to deal with my amends. By contrast, community justice would require that all parties be held.

There is a final fundamental flaw in the recovery community that is both a cause of great harm and a productive source of knowledge. It is that, while the programme actively encourages genuine accountability to people outside the community, seeking accountability from those within the community can be difficult. Sexual misconduct is regularly overlooked, and addicts with long periods of sobriety are too often venerated and met with deference when they cause harm. I've sat through instances of racism, misogyny, homophobia and transphobia in meetings knowing that there's little to no point in raising a concern because the group would not be capable of hearing it, let alone doing anything about it. Instead, I've chosen to avoid the same groups in future, which I am only able to do because London is so large and there are enough meetings to facilitate this.

The source of these problems is, of course, power. Outside of our recovery community, many of us lack the protections of wealth and prestige, but within the community there are opportunities to accumulate power. This is tied to the small size of recovery groups, the essential role that the community plays in treating our mental health, and the vulnerability of those who enter, along with the structure of sponsorship, the widespread reverence for those with long periods of sober time, and the immense popularity that individual members can and do amass. All this can be wielded to hide from the vulnerability of accountability.

The sponsor I describe above, the first person to walk me through my transformative justice process, was the same white woman who openly shared her racist beliefs with me as part of a misguided effort towards her own development in recovery. She also used to inadvertently offer me 'spiritual' advice that affirmed the humanity of people who had been racist to me over my own humanity. I endured this for over a year, largely because I was desperate. But once I hit eight months sober, I decided I was safe enough to ask her to discuss her racism with me in more sensitive terms, instead of demanding that I empathise in the ways that she expected me to. Although it wasn't an overt demand for accountability, it was met with cruelty and the assertion that my very desire to bring this up was evidence that I was not working my programme correctly and should expect to relapse soon.

We parted ways, but I see her response reflected often in the community. As a sponsor now myself, I do everything I can to eliminate power dynamics with my sponsees, but these dynamics inevitably exist, particularly with sponsees who have yet to get sober. I can see how easy it would be for me to hide behind that power (a power I otherwise lack in my day-to-day life) if they chose to call me out for harmful behaviour. I've felt a similar power when I've held group committee positions, and even with only four years' sobriety, I sometimes sense it when I talk to someone with significantly less sober time.

In short, the same dynamics that prevent accountability in the wider world recreate themselves in my recovery community. Those of us invested in transformative justice carve out our own spaces where we attempt to practise it, largely in meetings specifically for women and non-binary people, people of colour, and queer people. I can't say my contributions to those spaces have been perfect, but our collective attempts have created sites of recovery that I've found to be transformative. In these pockets, I've been able to deepen my commitments to a life lived with integrity while developing practical tools for how to build it.

It seems counterintuitive to suggest that such a contradictory community, ruled by genuinely successful principles of transformative justice yet practising them so inconsistently, could have anything to contribute to abolitionist futures. But it's productive to examine these contradictions and to remember that even imperfect communities straining towards a different vision for the world can offer us suggestions as we engage in the speculative practice of abolition. Ultimately, this community only offers pieces of the future. But they are, I think, revolutionary.

AFTERLIFE

I'm thinking of Martin O'Brien's 2021 performance art piece at the Institute of Contemporary Arts in London, *The Last Breath Society (Coughing Coffin)*. As someone whose cystic fibrosis diagnosis guaranteed a life expectancy of no more than thirty, which he then surpassed, O'Brien sought to understand the experience of living beyond the point when we are told we will die. He named the time that he now occupies, of life after one's expected death, 'zombie time'.[1]

I was drawn to O'Brien's work in the way I'm drawn to all stories of disabled people exceeding their life expectancies. In the months before I got sober, I knew alcoholism was going to kill me. Not in the I'll-die-if-I-don't-stop sense. In the I've-resigned-myself-to-waiting-for-death sense, because I'd been trying to stop for years and it was apparent that it wasn't going to happen. And then it did. And I continue to find my presence this far into the future jarring.

Like O'Brien, my relationship to mortality has changed, although I think less about waiting for death or about the embodiment of death in life than he does. Rather, I see myself as occupying an afterlife.

The shift from dying to not-dying was abrupt. Mainly because it was brought about by the sudden loss of cravings for alcohol, an embodied experience that gave me the space I needed to lay down the foundation of my recovery. Material improvements to my life appeared almost immediately, and while emotional growth has been and continues to be gradual, it feels accurate to say I died a death on 13 April 2019 and popped up in this new life on the fourteenth. In fact, many addicts in recovery speak of experiencing two separate lives in one—one before recovery and one after.

For me, this conception of the afterlife exists as a part of crip time. It is another way that the eschatological illusion of wholeness is shattered, because I continue to be very much disabled even in this afterlife.

My crip afterlife also complicates the eschatological mirage of transcendence, when a broken world is left behind for paradise. If anything, life before recovery was filled with attempts at transcendence, while the sobriety required for this afterlife has slammed me fully and inescapably into the material, psychically and relationally.

Even secularism deals in myths about the kind of transcendence that seeks to leave the world untouched. Here, transcendence appears as biopolitical projects that create an archetype of the 'normal' body, the model of health to which we should all aspire, unmarked by the disabling ravages of capitalism, unhindered by embodied restrictions.

In spiritual terms, as Sharon V. Betcher writes, 'Christianity as a philosophical deep materialism believes in this world, not in some other heaven beyond.'[2] So, I choose to use my crip afterlife to sit with the turmoil of this world's becoming, trying to enact specific political commitments rooted in justice for this world's oppressed.

There is, of course, also a long, fraught history when it comes to black Christians and the transcendent afterlife. Beginning with the trans-Atlantic slave trade and carrying on up to the present day, white supremacist theology has called for our acceptance of racism's apocalyptic horrors, the reward for which is admittance to a heaven without suffering. White missionaries began that call, pushing a 'futuristic eschatology', as black theologian James Cone describes it, in order to subdue slaves' desires for freedom.[3] But it went on to be picked up by conservative black church ministers, who preach that this suffering is redemptive but only if endured patiently and in anticipation of a happier afterlife.

Much has been done by Cone and other black theologians to challenge this justification for political inertia. What a black, crip eschatology has to offer is the question, 'what happens if you get to the afterlife and things are still quite shit?' A crip afterlife is one where the same oppressive forces that sought to kill us and failed persist. No reward has been provided for my suffering. Instead, in recovery I've been given an opportunity to contribute to doing something about those oppressive forces.

When the promise that the suffering of the oppressed is salvific is discovered to be hollow, we cannot be subdued with the hope of a happy afterlife. Those of us inhabiting a crip afterlife can carry on the work of being in the world in order to help enact God's will for it. We can report back to others the lie of the eschatological illusion.

Of course, the belief in an afterlife that offers respite from pain, that fulfils our deepest desires, is not inherently anti-thetical to revolutionary action. Nor is there only one form of engagement with the material that is conducive to radical thought. One can, for example, try to transcend the physical world in the process of changing it.

What comes to mind most often for me is the example of Haitian revolutionaries during the battle of Croix-des-Bou-quets in March 1792. How they rushed towards French forces without fear and pushed their hands into the mouths of enemy cannons to pull the bullets out because they knew that if they died they would reawaken in Africa. Guided by an African spiritual epistemology that, according to Marxist scholar Cedric Robinson, 'granted supremacy to metaphysics not the material', these enslaved revolutionaries believed that after death would come rebirth in the home from which they had been stolen.[4] This belief enabled them to call out to their comrades, 'Come, come we have them,' even with their arms inside cannons. In the account by historian C.L.R. James, 'Nothing could stop their devotion, and after six hours the troops of Port-au-Prince retired in disorder.'[5]

Two thousand Haitian soldiers died that day, while only a hundred of their opponents were killed. But according to Robinson, the revolutionaries 'were doubly blessed: they won the battle and even their dead were free'.[6] Toussaint Louverture and Jean-Jacques Dessalines, the two most prominent leaders of the Haitian Revolution, went on to lead these soldiers to form the world's first black republic in 1804, becoming the first nation to abolish slavery in the western hemisphere.

In allowing my faith to be inspired by this West African spiritual epistemology, I see that the problem is not the idea of a beautiful afterlife or belief in rebirth. It is the pleasant eschatological illusions that are crafted specifically to suppress the masses.

I see black crip eschatology as part of the legacy of black theologians like James Cone, who speak back to the futuristic eschatology of white missionaries and their heirs, rejecting transcendence when it means abandoning the world as we find it. The future promise of what we call the kin-dom of God is not for reward or retribution of wrongdoers but is a way of becoming unsatisfied with the present, empowering us to act to change it—to make the future now. Cone identified the Black Power movement that was flourishing in 1960s America as one way of achieving this. Looking to a future in which the God-given humanity of black people would be recognised, Christians committed to black liberation would understand that it was their moral duty to realise this future in their present historical moment by any means necessary.

This is a crip endeavour, too. The afterlife is always designated as future. A future in which everything we long for is, magically, already present. To inhabit a crip afterlife where pain and oppression continue to exist is to understand that the future must be intentionally built, and that it must be built today.

SARAH IS READING A POEM IN THE SOAS STUDENTS' UNION

Sarah is reading a poem in the SOAS Students' Union. She is standing at a microphone, notebook in hand, and a yellow light shines on her. I'm generally indifferent to poetry because of its opacity but, in that moment, I understand her. She's worked that magic that turns murky affect into clear spring water. I feel it hit me in the centre of my chest. I think I actually gasp. I hear a deep and gentle ripple behind me, turn my head to the left to see how the rest of the room is reacting just in time to see that we have all been caught up in the same swell. The swell of an unbroken wave that lifts you inches off the ocean floor, then sets you down again as it rolls gratefully to shore. Everyone's gaze is on Sarah, and I turn back to the stage convinced that we, her entire audience, are breathing to the same rhythm. It is the first time ever that I have felt the matter on the surface of my skin reach out to its kindred matter everywhere. The first time in a long time that I have felt a connection to the world unmediated by anxiety, artificial sentimentality, booze or dopamine. I have no desire to cling to it or make it last. It passes, like all things do.

ACKNOWLEDGEMENTS

I'm indebted to my first readers. Vera Chapiro Bernal, thank you for encouraging me to write more bravely. Miriam Gauntlett, it is an honour to be your comrade and to be read by you. Heather Abbey, thank you for patiently holding my anxieties about the book with me and for showing me how to celebrate its completion.

To Lola Olufemi and Christine Pungong, for letting me burst into your rooms at all hours of the day and night to bounce ideas off you.

To the friends and family that have encouraged and supported me throughout: Susie Sebatindira, Sandy O., Lee Byrne, Arenike Adebajo, Lydia Ramah, Bennie Maisano, Maria Smickersgill, Bridie Murphy, Harry Read, Micha Frazer-Carroll, Suhaiymah Manzoor-Khan, Christie Costello, Sarah Lasoye, Rosie Agnew, Len Zachariou, Joshi Gottlieb, Han Stephens, Parwana Haydar, Venetia Iga, Lorraine, Mae, Karen, Savannah and Selam.

And to Farhaana Arefin and Brekhna Aftab, for trusting me with this opportunity and for drawing out the heart of the book during the editing process.

NOTES

Introduction

1   Robert McRuer, *Crip Times: Disability, Globalization, and Resistance*, New York, NY: New York University Press, 2018, p. 19.

2   Jack Halberstam, *In a Queer Time and Place: Transgender Bodies, Subcultural Lives*, New York, NY: New York University Press, 2005.

3   From Katherine McKittrick's phrase 'black livingness', in *Dear Science and Other Stories*, Durham, NC: Duke University Press, 2021.

Memory Failures

1   Ursula K. Le Guin, *Always Coming Home*, London: Orion, 2016, p. 244.

Sober Failures

1   Jack Halberstam, *The Queer Art of Failure*, Durham, NC & London: Duke University Press, 2011, p. 27.

2   *Ibid.*, p. 29.

3   *Ibid.*, p. 154.

4 Eli Clare, *Brilliant Imperfection: Grappling with Cure*, Durham, NC: Duke University Press, 2017.

5 Lisa Fannen, *Warp & Weft: Psycho-Emotional Health, Politics and Experiences*, London: Active Distribution, 2021.

Is Addiction a Disability?

1 Alison Kafer, *Feminist, Queer, Crip*, Bloomington, IN: Indiana University Press, 2013, p. 8.

2 Laura Mills, 'Acknowledging the Plight of Pain Patients in the US', *Human Rights Watch*, 29 April 2019, https://www.hrw.org/news/2019/04/29/acknowledging-plight-pain-patients-us, accessed 7 March 2023.

3 Kojo Koram (ed.), *The War on Drugs and the Global Colour Line*, London: Pluto Press, 2019, pp. 11–16.

4 Troy Farah, 'People with Chronic Pain Will Protest the CDC's Crackdown on Opioids', *Vice*, 5 April 2018, https://www.vice.com/en/article/wj7zyz/pain-patient-rally, accessed 30 January 2023.

5 Johanna Hedva, 'Letter to a Young Doctor', *Triple Canopy*, 17 January 2018, https://canopycanopycanopy.com/contents/letter-to-a-young-doctor, accessed 30 January 2023.

6 Equality Act 2010 Guidance, https://assets.publishing.service.gov.uk/government/uploads/system/uploads/attachment_data/file/570382/Equality_Act_2010-disability_definition.pdf, accessed 30 January 2023.

7 Marta Russell, *Capitalism and Disability: Selected Writings by Marta Russell*, ed. Keith Rosenthal, Chicago, IL: Haymarket Books, 2019, Kindle Locations 407–8.

8 Karl Marx, *Capital: Volumes One and Two*, Ware: Wordsworth Editions Limited, 2013, p. 674.

9   Beatrice Adler-Bolton & Artie Vierkant, *Health Communism: A Surplus Manifesto*, Brooklyn, NY: Verso Books, 2022, pp. 5–6.

Ambivalence

1   Nick Riotfag, *Towards a Less Fucked Up World: Sobriety and Anarchist Struggle*, Chico, CA: AK Press, 2015.

2   Eli Clare, 'Stolen Bodies, Reclaimed Bodies: Disability and Queerness', *Public Culture* 13:3, September 2001, p. 364, https://doi.org/10.1215/08992363-13-3-359.

3   Leah Lakshmi Piepzna-Samarasinha, *Care Work: Dreaming Disability Justice*, Vancouver: Arsenal Pulp Press, 2018, p. 81.

Loneliness

1   Marjorie Hewitt Suchocki, *God Christ Church: A Practical Guide to Process Theology*, New York, NY: The Crossroad Publishing Company, 1989, p. 51.

2   *Ibid.*, p. 55.

3   *Ibid.*, p. 51.

4   *Ibid.*, p. 57.

5   *Ibid.*

6   *Ibid.*, p. 54.

Alcoholics and the Imago Dei

1   Joan Tollifson, 'Imperfection Is a Beautiful Thing: On Disability and Meditation', in Kenny Fries (ed.), *Staring Back: The Disability Experience from the Inside Out*, New York, NY: Plume, 1997, p. 110.

2   Sharon V. Betcher, *Spirit and the Politics of Disablement*, Minneapolis, MN: Fortress Press, 2007, Kindle Location 2155.

3   Luke 6:20–21.

4   Luke 6:24–25.

5   Diane di Prima, *Revolutionary Letters*, London: Silver Press, 2021, p. 20.

6   Betcher, *op. cit.*, Kindle Location 83.

A Black Feminist God

1   'Racism is the state-sanctioned and/or extralegal production and exploitation of group-differentiated vulnerability to premature death.' Ruth Wilson Gilmore, *Golden Gulag: Prisons, Surplus, Crisis, and Opposition in Globalizing California*, Berkeley, CA: University of California Press, 2007, p. 274.

2   Audre Lorde, *A Burst of Light: And Other Essays*, Mineola, NY: Ixia Press, 2017, Kindle Locations 1258–69.

Abolition

1   Survey of 2,090 UK adults carried out on behalf of the Royal Society for Public Health by Populus, 12–14 February 2016, https://www.rsph.org.uk/static/uploaded/68d93cdc-292c-4a7b-babfc0a8ee252bc0.pdf.

2   Simon Woolley, 'Our drug laws are racist, and doctors must speak out – an essay by Simon Woolley', *The BMJ* 374:2147, September 2021, https://doi.org/10.1136/bmj.n2147.

3   Michael Shiner, Zoe Carre, Rebekah Delsol & Niamh Eastwood, 'The Colour of Injustice: 'Race', Drugs and Law Enforcement in England and Wales', StopWatch, Release & The International Drug Policy Unit, London School of Economics, 2018, https://www.lse.ac.uk/united-states/Assets/Documents/The-Colour-of-Injustice.pdf.

4   Woolley, *op. cit.*

5   Transform Drug Policy Foundation, 'The Misuse of Drugs Act: A Short History', https://transformdrugs.org/mda-at-50/a-short-history-of-the-misuse-of-drugs-act, accessed 26 February 2023.

6   Edward White, 'Unspeakable Affections', *The Paris Review*, 5 May 2017, https://www.theparisreview.org/blog/2017/05/05/unspeakable-affections, accessed 26 February 2023.

7   Kojo Koram, 'Introduction', and Elise Wohlbold & Dawn Moore, 'Benevolent whiteness in Canadian drug regulation', in Kojo Koram (ed.), *The War on Drugs and the Global Colour Line*, London: Pluto Press, 2019, pp. 15, 28–29.

8   White, *op. cit.*

9   Alex Brown, 'Cannabis in the 1950s British Tabloids', *Points*, 10 September 2020, https://pointshistory.com/2020/09/10/cannabis-in-the-1950s-british-tabloids, accessed 26 February 2023.

10   'The Misuse of Drugs Act: A Short History'.

11   Tobi Thomas, 'Opiates drive drug deaths to record level in England and Wales', *The Guardian*, 3 August 2022, https://www.theguardian.com/society/2022/aug/03/cocaine-and-opiates-drive-record-high-drug-deaths-in-england-and-wales, accessed 26 February 2023.

12   John Collins, 'The Irish Experience: Policy Transfer from US Drug Courts', in John Collins, Winifred Agnew-Pauley & Alexander

Soderholm (eds), *Rethinking Drug Courts: International Experiences of a US Policy Export*, London: London Publishing Partnership, 2019, pp. 70–1.

13 James L. Nolan Jr, *Legal Accents, Legal Borrowing: The International Problem-Solving Court Movement*, Princeton, NJ: Princeton University Press, 2009, p. 130.

14 Collins, *op. cit.*, p. 70.

15 Tanzil Chowdhury, 'Policing the "Black party": racialized drugs policing at festivals in the UK', in Kojo Koram (ed.), *The War on Drugs and the Global Colour Line*, London: Pluto Press, 2019, p. 54.

16 Harm Reduction International, 'Illegal Smile: The Political Economy of Drug-Induced Pleasure', *YouTube*, 4 April 2022, https://www.youtube.com/watch?v=7AMt25a3kUM&t=4118s, accessed 26 February 2023.

Accountability

1 Liat Ben-Moshe, *Decarcerating Disability: Deinstitutionalization and Prison Abolition*, Minneapolis, MN & London: University of Minnesota Press, 2020, p. 31.

2 Mariame Kaba, *We Do This 'Til We Free Us: Abolitionist Organizing and Transformative Justice*, Chicago, IL: Haymarket Books, 2021, p. 137.

3 *Ibid.*

4 Adrian Horton, 'A life in quotes: bell hooks', *The Guardian*, 15 December 2021, https://www.theguardian.com/books/2021/dec/15/bell-hooks-best-quotes-feminism-race, accessed 26 February 2021.

Afterlife

1   Martin O'Brien, 'You are my death: the shattered temporalities of zombie time', *Wellcome Open Research*, 5:135, June 2020, https://doi.org/10.12688/wellcomeopenres.15966.1.

2   Sharon V. Betcher, *Spirit and the Politics of Disablement*, Minneapolis, MN: Fortress Press, 2007, Kindle Locations 398–9.

3   James H. Cone, *Black Theology and Black Power*, New York, NY: Orbis Books, 2021, p. 114.

4   Cedric J. Robinson, *Black Marxism: The Making of the Black Radical Tradition*, Chapel Hill, NC: The University of North Carolina Press, 1983, p. 169.

5   C.L.R. James, *The Black Jacobins: Toussaint L'Ouverture and the San Domingo Revolution*, New York, NY: Vintage Books, 1989, pp. 108–9.

6   Robinson, *op. cit.*, p. 170.